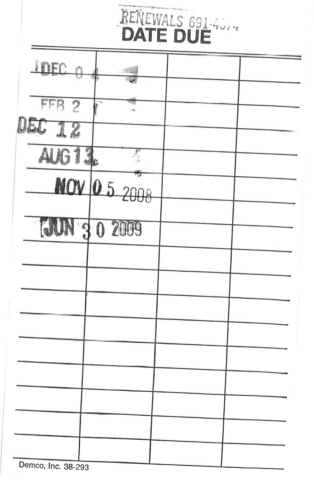

RENEWALS 691-45??

DATE DUE

DEC 0 4			
FEB 2			
DEC 12			
AUG 13			
NOV 0 5 2008			
JUN 3 0 2009			

Demco, Inc. 38-293

The
Raft
Is
Not
the
Shore

Daniel Berrigan / *Thich Nhat Hanh*

The
Raft
Is
Not
the
Shore

CONVERSATIONS TOWARD A BUDDHIST/CHRISTIAN AWARENESS

Beacon
Press
Boston

Copyright © 1975 by Daniel Berrigan, S. J.
and Thich Nhat Hanh

Woodcuts copyright © 1974 by Vo-Dinh,
reproduced by permission of The Loa Binh Press

Beacon Press books are published under the auspices
of the Unitarian Universalist Association

Published simultaneously in hardcover and paperback editions

All rights reserved

Printed in the United States of America

9   8   7   6   5   4   3   2   1

Library of Congress Cataloging in Publication Data

Berrigan, Daniel.
    The raft is not the shore.
    1. Religion—Addresses, essays, lectures.
I. Nhat Hanh, Thich, joint author.   II. Title.
BL50.B46   200   75–5287
ISBN 0–8070–1124–X
ISBN 0–8070–1125–8 (pbk.)

Contents

The
Raft
Is
Not
the
Shore

1

Memory,
Eucharist,
Death

BERRIGAN: The notion of remembrance has always been fascinating to me. People seldom think of the memory as a creative power—one that brings together different senses of time, or keeps one from merely floating in a round and ricocheting off other people and events. As a surgeon would, we "re-member" an amputee or a broken body or a skeleton. It means that we put broken lives together, into one body. The ability also to draw upon the future, to re-member the future, is, it seems to me, a very rich notion; so many people have the idea that memory is merely dredging up the past. And, especially in the sense of affliction, a down-putting, the memory of past wrong, of death, of separation of families, of personal humiliations. Few people have their lives so articulated that memory can gaze on the future with equanimity, simply because their present is quite intense and quite—even quite joyous.

This idea struck me in thinking about Martin Luther King and his attitude toward his own people. Even though there were the bitterest memories of bondage and enslavement, the people could arise and create a human future in the midst of their oppression. In some mysterious way the bitter and unpromising past had been transformed into a vision—a vision of an entirely new future. And the most stunning fact of all was that the struggle—the exodus as the Bible says—also included the keeper, the slave master. He was never left behind.

The same exodus, of course, had to be seen in an entirely different light by whites. The question for King was, How do we cease being slaves? But the question for whites is, How do we cease being slave masters? It's easy to see one form of enslavement if one has experienced it; but it's very difficult to see the other, you know? The possessors of the earth, at least according to the Bible, very seldom change. It's a greater miracle than when the sinner repents or one of the lepers is healed or when the blind are given sight. We don't hear that many of the Jewish Sanhedrin or Roman curia or that a Pilate are converted or attain a new vision or illumination. Literally, they seem in the Bible to have no future; the future always belongs to the remnant which has come out of slavery. These are very disturbing messages about consciousness.

NHAT HANH: I wasn't thinking of the same meaning of the word *re-member*. In French they have the word *recueillement* to describe the attitude of someone trying to be himself, not to be dispersed, one member of the body here, another there. One tries to recover, to be once more in good shape, to become whole again.

And I think that is the beginning of awakening. People speak about sudden enlightenment. It is not something very difficult to understand; each of us has undergone that kind of experience in our own life, several times in our own life. The distance separating forgetfulness, ignorance, and enlightenment—that distance is short; it is so short that it is no distance at all. One may be ignorant now, but he can be enlightened in the next second. The recovering of oneself can be realized in just one portion of one second. And to be aware of who we are, what we are, what we are doing, what we are thinking, seems to be a very easy thing to do—and yet it is the most important thing: *se recueillir*—the starting point of the salvation of oneself.

One time I meditated on the meaning of the Eucharist. Suddenly I found that message of Jesus so clear. The disciples had been following Him and had seen Him, had the chance to look at Him, to look in His eyes, to see Him smile, to see Him in reality. But it seems to me that they were not capable of being in real contact with that marvelous reality. Then He broke bread and poured the wine and said, "This is My flesh, My blood. Drink it, take it, eat it, and you will have life eternal." I think the message is so clear, so clear to a Buddhist monk. We eat a lot, we drink a lot; but what do we eat? We eat phantoms; we drink ghosts. We don't eat real bread—reality. We don't drink real wine. But if Jesus said, "This is My flesh, this is My blood," it's a very drastic way of awakening man from forgetfulness, from ignorance.

So, I think, when you perform the rite of Eucharist, you have a role that is very similar to the act of Jesus. Your role is to bring back life and reality to a community that is participating in the worship. There have been times when I was not able to see that awakening happening in the Eucharist. Then I said, "There must be something wrong. It's not because you perform the correct act and say the correct words that a miracle happens. No. You have to be able to awaken reality, to bring back reality. And that depends on who you are as a person, depends on your being *life*."

One time I spoke at a Buddhist meeting; I said, "In order to save the world, each of us has to build a pagoda."

BERRIGAN: To build a pagoda?

NHAT HANH: Yes. To build a pagoda. There were people who thought that I was urging them to build more pagodas so Buddhism would become a national religion. But this pagoda cannot be built by stones and sticks and things like that, because this pagoda is a sanctuary where you have a chance to be alone and to face yourself, the reality of yourself. If you don't have a pagoda like that to go into each day, several times each day, then you cannot protect the Eucharist, you cannot protect yourself, and you cannot protect the world from destruction. You were saying?

BERRIGAN: The Eucharist brings to mind the death of Jesus. We are talking during Holy Week, and one question keeps haunting us. How did this man live; how did He die?

The Gospels seem to hint that He knew what was coming —that He went into it freely, beginning with that anguished episode in Gethsemane. John is quite remote and spiritualized in his descriptions. Luke, being a physician as the tradition said, was close to the physical aspects. He is the only one of the evangelists who gives such a detail as the sweat of blood. This is evidently connected with His submitting to and overcoming the fear of death—death by anticipation.

John seems to say that Jesus saw the other side of death, while Luke stresses the agony involved in death itself. So Luke tells us He sweated blood; and John says He met some pilgrims and told a parable. You have almost a loss of control on one side and complete control on the other. Luke says His sweat came down like blood, like drops of blood. And John says that in the midst of His struggle He held a quiet discussion, speaking to some gentiles about a grain of wheat falling to the ground and dying and then rising again—as though He was indeed talking about Himself.

I think that in both instances we have a rush of anguish—the agony of the person who has lost everything, but still must lose himself. There's no doubt that Jesus lived as though possessions were not entities with a life of their own, but were objects, were instrumental. He walked through a great many of them, enjoying them, using them, but never really attached them to Himself, like a string of tin cans. Life itself was something else. At the end of His life came a great fear of death, as though to say to us that anyone who loves life deeply enters into the injustice and violence of undeserved death with dread —dread for the loss of his bodily integrity, his whole sense of the world. One's own life is that last and dearest possession of all. And now He must go; life itself must be given up. This rhythm of agony recurs three times: Luke says Jesus prays and looks for help, goes back to pray and looks for help, and then prays. Then He walks to His captors.

My brief experience in prison included death—a rehearsal of death. You could not come out of this experience unchanged, I think, unless you were very heedless while you went through it. But, it's interesting; we're never told in the New Testament not to fear death. Nor are we even told that fear of death is un-natural; maybe that's a better way of putting it. But we're al-

ways told that there is a greater encounter for us, a counter-
poise to fear. I think that the hint is always there that actuality
is much less fearful than fear itself. In prison, I found, when I
nearly died one day, that suddenly knowing I was dying was a
very quiet and simple moment; and there was no fear.

NHAT HANH: Maybe because, at that moment, there is an
awareness that what you have thought of as death is not death.
And maybe you have the realization that if one doesn't know
how to die, then he doesn't know how to live either. It seems
to me that in the Christian scriptures we can distinguish two
kinds of death. The first kind of death I would propose that we
write with a small "d." It is part of life; without it there is no
life. The other kind of Death is in contrast to life; it is real
Death. So dying, as many of us experience, is just a form of
living. It is not difficult for us to see that if there is no death,
then life cannot be possible. Life is a process of change, and
change brings birth and death. How can there be birth if death
does not exist?

To speak from the standpoint of Buddhist scriptures, ours is
a doctrine of *emptiness.* But emptiness is not annihilation or
anything like that; emptiness is a means of perceiving the
nature of reality. In the *Heart Sutra,* a text which we read
several times every day, it is said that after we have perceived
the emptiness of things, we can overcome all kinds of fear and
suffering, including the fear of death. Our meditation on the
emptiness of things is to help us see, to realize the close relationship between phenomena. Life is a phenomenon, death is a
phenomenon, and both together are life. And that is why when
one has seen the real nature of things, he will acquire a kind of
fearlessness—an attitude of calm—because he knows his death
will bring no end to life. He knows too that his existing does
not depend on his "being alive" now. So the existence of reality
transcends both what we call life and death. Only the lack of
awakening, the lack of awareness of reality, might be called
real Death. But once you are awake to realities, what we usually call death is only part of life.

BERRIGAN: Yes, yes. While you spoke I was reminded of our
scriptures, especially of the attitude of Jesus toward death,

according to John's Gospel. John uses the word *death* remarkably few times; and as far as I can recall the word is never used
by Jesus in speaking of Himself. He always uses a kind of
paraphrase for that word. Maybe because there are so many
things that the word *death* blocks off, because it has the popular notion of extinction or the notion of personified reality or
of a malignant power at large in the world. Men pay tribute to
it, make an idol of it. But Jesus uses phrases like, "If I be lifted
up, I will draw all things to Myself"; or, "I will go to the
Father"; or, "I pass out of this world to the Father." In the
Greek text there's a play on the word *pass*, the Greek equivalent for the Hebrew word *Pasch*. The paschal mystery is the
passage out of slavery, out of Egypt. It's almost as though He's
saying, "If I pass out of Egypt into freedom, that's My notion
of death." It's a remarkably rich kind of imagery, meant, I
think, to cut off brutally and suddenly our age-old tribute to
death, which the world is always exacting—and is always
paying too, because to exact is to pay.

In Paul's letters the notion of death is also very powerful
and dramatic. "If death abounds, then life abounds more fully"
—you know the two are in contest. The other writers treat the
death of Jesus gently, biologically even. From an apologetic
point of view, they are anxious to convey that Jesus really underwent this: that His soul left His body, that He truly became one with the inert world and then arose, that there's no
fraud, that He truly died.

I think it's a very interesting balance for John to say, "Death
has not much power over us"; and for the others to say, "Yes,
but we really die." Do you know what I mean? Jesus died. And
the interception of this cruel cycle doesn't begin until He sub-
mits. He says, "Into Thy hands I commend My spirit." And
then He expires. Only then does the Father intervene—afterward. But He does not intervene to save Jesus from death: "No,
no, let it all go. Let it happen."

NHAT HANH: In ancient Buddhist monastic circles they used
to speak of *the most important problem*: the problem of life
and death. And it was often reported that the monk who was
enlightened most of the time just smiled, as if he were someone

who had been searching for something and had suddenly found that he had not lost that something—it was in his pocket all the time.

Many treatises were written, dealing with death. They say before you die, you do not die; while you are alive, death does not exist; and after you die, death does not exist either. Before death, there is no death; and after death there is no death. Something like that. It's nice!

BERRIGAN: I remember once Merton discussing this question of death with the novices. He spoke with joy, almost with anticipation, of death. He said the only thing that relieved the life of a monk from absolute absurdity was that his life was a joyful conquest of death. And that life made sense only because the monk had conquered death. He was living apart from a world which paid death such tribute—racist, violent, militaristic—a kind of taxation exacted on people by death itself. You could sense in the words and the way he spoke and the lightness of his tone that he had made it—that he had really conquered this thing.

His death followed shortly. And while it was heartbreaking for his friends, it was beautiful to hear him facing it in that spirit. So, I think for us it is a great joy, a great privilege, to live a life of faith in which the possibility of the conquest of death is in our midst everyday. I have the impression that Merton was able to create that spirit among the younger monks. There was an enlightenment in his habitual attitude toward people, toward fame, toward—I don't know—whatever the opposite of idolatries is. He had a true sense of God and the world, and I think people came from him with a sense of the possibilities which life held—enlightenment maybe. I think this was because he had gotten rid of so much death in his own makeup.

NHAT HANH: I think it is possible to say that eternal life is the kind of life that includes death. In fact, eternal life without death is not possible. For example, you have a coin, a piece of money. You have two sides, and one side is the opposite of the other. But this side is not the coin. The other side is not the coin either. The coin is both. So I was talking of eternal life, the coin; and noneternal life is just one face of the two. Once you choose eternal life you choose death as well, and both are life. But if you want to take only one face of the coin, you don't have the coin.

BERRIGAN: In the States, so much of what we call daily life, human life, is concerned with death in a fashion that's very peculiar. For instance, we have all kinds of "wars" declared against this or that aspect of death. We have a war on poverty, a war on cancer, a war on heart disease. There's even a war on war. These aspects of death around us, within us, are always conceived of as the great enemy which must be overcome so that we can get beyond disease, war, poverty—into what they like to think of as the good life, the real life, the life which has no death within it. And this dream continues. But it's always a kind of troubled and violent dream because it implies (and sometimes says openly) that, in order to make that leap, we have to make war on something or on somebody. To attain anything like the truth of life, or a life with others, something is always in our way; and must be done away with, must be overcome.

Of course the fact is that the culture is almost totally bankrupt of a vision of what a good life might be. We're ridden by consumerism, fear, violence, racism—all these terrible mythologies which forever put off any real vision. I find it interesting in the light of scripture that, while the dream of the good life is forever delayed, death is always magnified: omnipresent, omnivorous, the shadowy other, the enemy. So we never really pay tribute to life at all, and never arrive at life. What we're really doing all the time is paying tribute to death. The eventuality of life is put off and put off and put off, because the obstacles and enemies multiply like piranhas, forever.

Until the end of history we'll be waging a shadow war. The shadows are created by our own psyche in the image of death. In this itch for beatitude, which has nothing to do with God or our neighbor—in order to get nearer to that, we must kill all the time. In the pursuit of life, we are always dealing out death. War becomes the continual occupation and preoccupation in the minds of people who are purportedly trying to get to a better life.

Speaking in biblical terms, God is superseded by the ape of God, which is actually personified death. This is the shrine at which we worship. This, I think, is the practical consequence of our war on life. Our real shrines are nuclear installations and the Pentagon and the war research laboratories. This is where we worship, allowing ourselves to hear the obscene command that we kill and be killed. A command which, it seems to me, is anti-Christ, is anti-God, you know.

Someday you must take a trip into the countryside of North Dakota, just south of the Canadian border. It's all prairie; it's all flat. And for miles and miles on the horizon, the only visible thing is a nuclear installation, shaped like a pyramid. Most of it, of course, is subterranean. Someone told me that in Egypt the construction of the pyramids began just before the downfall of a dynasty. It was that kind of sarcophagus, that kind of a shrine to death, which they raised as an admission that they were dying. Someone said that if North Dakota seceded from the Union, it would be the third nuclear power. And this is a farming state.

NHAT HANH: So, war becomes the only possibility. During the periods when the war was very intensive in Vietnam, most of us meditated on death every day, because death was a matter of every second, every minute.

In that atmosphere, there was pressure on each one of us to work more quickly, to break through the problems of life and death. On one hand, we were pushed by the need to bring help to the suffering. You had to bury the dead and help the mutilated children, and often we were busy building shelters for others. You had to be busy all the time doing these things. But your mind was always on problems of life and death.

If death came and you were not prepared, you would not be able to take it well. But there was another stimulus and others acted quite differently. They said "Well, you don't know when you'll die, so if you have some money why not spend it?" That was another attitude, since the future was so insecure.

My Master died during the 1968 Tet offensive, but not from a bomb or a bullet. He couldn't stand it. He just couldn't stand it. He was old—eighty-five.

BERRIGAN: He couldn't stand—the war? The assaults on the monastery?

NHAT HANH: The monastery was struck by one mortar shell; but no one was killed. At that time I was not in the country; I did not have the opportunity to see him before he died.

I remember quite well what he said when I was a novice. It was a long time ago, during the French occupation. We had rice for the monks, and we had to bury the rice in order to preserve it because French soldiers came and stole it from us. We put it in big containers and buried them in the yard. One day he and a few of us novices went out to the yard to un-earth one can of rice for dinner. The Master was old, but he still followed our tradition that every monk works: "no work, no food." He said to us while he worked, "I'm so tired. Let's wait until after I die." We Vietnamese say, "Well, just wait until I'm dead, I won't be tired anymore." He was joking with us; all of us were sweating because of the hard work. I thought it was only a joke but half a minute later, he said to us, "Who will be the person after I am dead? Who will be the person who will not be tired?"

I was struck by that and I took it as a theme of meditation. It helped me a lot. I realized that it is by watching the Master, his way of living and listening, that you find the things that are useful for your own work. It's not by studying the scriptures hours and hours with explanations of a professor that you find those things. Now he's no more. He's no longer there, and I am supposed to succeed him. But since I am here, another disciple is in charge of the monastery.

BERRIGAN: We thank God you're here. And since it's the anniversary of Holy Thursday this week, maybe we can all celebrate the Eucharist. It would be marvelous.

NHAT HANH: Sure. We'll make some bread.

2

Religion
in
the
World

BERRIGAN: I think I would like to begin by saying a few things about people whom I met recently in the Middle East. These meetings opened the question of what it is to be religious in the world.

I was struck by two things. First, in Israel and elsewhere, the people who were thoughtful were antireligious. And the religious people we met were very closed in their suppositions about the state, in obedience to the state, and in violence. In no sense were they evil people, but they were convinced of one way of thinking, one way of acting, one attitude. They were offering very little resources in face of the suffering and the death of many innocent people. They were also convinced, to some degree at least, of the inevitability of violence.

So they found me suspect and treated me rather harshly. I regretted very often that there was so little religious sense available to deal with these terrifying human differences. I was only half-joking after one meeting in Jerusalem when I said that it was the religious people who gave us the hardest times of all, compared with the extreme rightists. I thought that that would be an important thing to try to understand—why this should be so.

NHAT HANH: Do you think that the sufferings have drawn

people nearer to each other? I mean people of different religions?

BERRIGAN: Not really; suffering has made them extremely rigid and reactionary. There is in Israel, for example, a very powerful political bloc to the right which is resisting any change, any lessening of militarization. Both sides, right and left, fear the religious people very much because they know that their influence, in the scale of political change, will be crucial. But to look on religion as some kind of a leaven, you know, of daring or of risk is almost unheard of. In the kibbutzim, for instance, they said, when we asked them, that they were antireligious. They felt that to be politically responsible they had to be so.

NHAT HANH: And so, on the right wing there are people who are using religion as a means to achieve strength by political unity. It is suggested that that kind of alliance will protect religion as well as people.

BERRIGAN: It's a very strange conception that religion, which is seen as a part of citizenship, is aligned to the most frightening kind of militarism, as well as to efforts to make the state more religious. The religious bloc resists the secular development of the state; it wants everybody to observe a close moral code in observance of Sabbath, dietary laws, or marriage laws. It evidently conceives of the state as a theocracy which is immersed in a sea of secularism, and it must resist this to preserve itself—and resist any possibility of living together and of welcoming Christians and Moslems and unbelieving people to an equal ground.

NHAT HANH: I wonder what the content of sermons would be, in weekly religious meetings? Would they preach about the necessity of protecting people who are united under that religion? Or would they also apeak about the spiritual dimension of life, religious principles of behavior as far as problems like killing, oppression, are concerned?

BERRIGAN: We didn't have a chance to attend any services. But the people that we met with impressed us with their view of common problems, their view of violence, the killing even of children. I recall their vengefulness, the kind of siege mentality which religion was fostering—that the Jew and his state are caught in the midst of essentially evil people who wish their destruction.

They are haunted by the Holocaust. This is very much part of it. They are determined that this will never happen again, and yet they feel it could happen again, any time. And the terriorists are always giving notice of that, you know, through attacks on schools and buses and settlements at the frontier. But, religion just seems to intensify the bad, bloody feelings of people and to give them a kind of blessing for feeling that way. I think such people read the Old Testament in the narrowest possible sense, as though God were a God of vengeance and wars were still religious ventures; it was a sacred thing to retaliate against the enemy—who is always accepted as the enemy. Any reconciliation work is ignored by religious people, almost unheard of. So, this is very sad.

NHAT HANH: In Israel, is there a minority who hold the Moslem belief?

BERRIGAN: A very small, unacceptable minority. I didn't get the impression that they were particularly religious or that they were offering much hope either. It seemed to me that here and there was a Christian, Jew, or Moslem, religious or secular, especially among young people, who was saying, "We must change, and any change in public must begin with ourselves." It was my first experience, I think, in any country where the religious voice was so negative. Not absent, but negative. It would almost be better if it were absent because then it wouldn't be offering a kind of divine sanction for continuing the killing.

NHAT HANH: And when you met and discussed with leaders of the Palestinian movements, did the problem of religious people arise?

BERRIGAN: Well, one had the impression that they were in no sense antireligious. They had great respect for us, for instance, as religious people involved in resistance in our own country. They spoke of that explicitly, and one got the impression that religious people were as acceptable to them as anyone else was, as long as they had something to offer. While we would not be sharing on the religious basis, they would offer cooperation to people who came to say, "We believe also that the state must grant you room, that your people must be accepted, and that a settlement must be reached for you." So, they had a kind of a classical secular view of religion, neither favorable nor hostile.

In the Arabic countries and in Israel, there's a great unspoken longing for someone who has the courage to say, "We must change and change rapidly; otherwise we all perish." However the feeling is one of mixed despair and shock and depression of spirit—a sense in Israel that they're not on the right track and haven't been for a long time, but don't know where the right track is. And that there are very few who can help.

NHAT HANH: Has there been any effort of religious people of both sides to meet and discuss the problems?

BERRIGAN: Well, we were the first in a long time to come into Israel and say to a rabbi, "We want to meet with some religious people. We feel it is important as outsiders to share with you our view of our struggle at home, as well as our view of the feelings of the Arabs especially the Palestinians, about Israel. We want to share this with religious people." So, a rabbi gathered six Jews, a Catholic, and a Protestant. They were mainly professors and chaplains. Well, it was the hardest evening of the whole trip.

NHAT HANH: They had never met Moslems of the Arab countries?

BERRIGAN: I think that this is almost unheard of. The only person we met who was doing reconciliation work was a Maronite priest, exiled by church authorities to a small Arab village about fifty miles from Tel Aviv. We heard about him on Cyprus. He is a brilliant young theologian and linguist who has spoken to audiences in Europe and in the States, and he always returns to this village, to build community. He invites Jewish students and professors to come and live with the people while they're having their discussions. "Go into the village please, and live with our people. Find out what they're like—that they're not monsters or enemies, that they're very

simple, beautiful, gentle, hard-working, poor people." He said
that change comes from living experience and an effort to
talk honestly. But it's very slow.

A rabbi, whom we both have met—you in Ceylon and I in
Jerusalem—was one of these visitors to the village. At one
point, the rabbi invited the priest in return to his own home.
After they had sat for a while and he had served coffee, the
rabbi finally confessed that in twenty-five years, this priest
was the first Arab, the first Palestinian, he had ever had
in his home. The priest couldn't believe it. He exploded, "You
mean that you have been teaching the Bible all these years and
had never had one of us into your house?" And the rabbi was
ashamed.

NHAT HANH: Did you notice anything on the part of the
rabbis you talked to—any sign that they felt they were caught
between religious ideals and the necessity of preserving Israel
as a nation-state?

BERRIGAN: I speak only of an impression, but it seems to me
that in some cases a genuine religious understanding gets lost,
you know. After a while, under these extreme crises, living so
long in an atmosphere of violence, the religious person may
think he retains a religious attitude. But, in reality, he has the
same attitude as the state. Still, he speaks in a religious language. It's very difficult to get beyond that language and to
help probe his real thinking, the real strata, the drives that lie
beyond religious metaphors, religious symbols, religious cere-
monies. I deeply believe that at heart, when religious people
accede to violence, they become worldly, violence-oriented
persons who now can invoke a religious excuse for being that
way. But the fact is that, in one way or another, the state has
come to embody the religious hope. The state is the expression
of the religious community; the army is the natural protector
of the religious community. The need for retaliation is, after a
while, a religious need. The situation might change if such
people can sense the distance they have moved from a religious
vision, acting and living and teaching this way.

NHAT HANH: In that case, religion plays only the role of an
ideology to preserve the identity of a race, of a nation, of a

group of people. But I think that any genuine religious life must express reverence toward life, nonviolence, communion between man and man, man and the absolute. You met in Tel Aviv a rabbi, a professor of scripture, whom I met in Ceylon?

BERRIGAN: Yes.

NHAT HANH: In Colombo, we talked for a long time. Then he asked me this question: "What would you do if you were in my position?" I told him that was a very hard question because the most I could do was to imagine that I was in his position, but imagination is not the real thing. So I said, "What I can tell you is how the Buddhists in similar conditions behaved in the past."

For instance, in India in the ninth century, Hindus and Moslems undertook a great persecution of Buddhism. They burned down Buddhist temples and killed monks and destroyed scriptures. What the Buddhist monks did in those days was to flee to Nepal, where they preserved their manuscripts. They couldn't carry the Buddha statues, which were magnificent, with them. But they did carry the scriptures. After that, Buddhism flourished in Asia—in Tibet and China and Japan. Theirs was a kind of negative resistance.

But if they had organized violent resistance and killed Moslems and Hindus, I don't think that would have been real Buddhist behavior. By organizing violent resistance, they might have preserved something that is called Buddhism, but might not be Buddhist at all in substance. By acting in the way they did, they preserved the identity of Buddhism.

I also asked him whether he thought Israel as a *nation* is the most important condition for the existence of the Jewish people, even when in order to protect that nation it is necessary to bomb people, to destroy life in order to protect life. A contradiction in itself. I suggested that there may be ways other than the killing of people to protect life.

BERRIGAN: I had a sense of a kind of strange ecumenism in listening to such talk. Because I think this attitude, "kill now and pay later" or "kill now and save later," is by no means confined to any one group. I had been in Northern Ireland and seen Christians killing one another with great enthusiasm.

And I had a sense of being at home, in the United States, where in the last decade the official Church has played this same game.

I think there's a wave passing over the world—a wave of blood, of utter moral irresponsibility toward others. In such circumstances, one recognizes two things. First, that there's a diabolic ecumenism at work. The main-line religions have joined this effort to make killing acceptable and normal—at least by silence. Usually there is some kind of an obsession with their own well being. And then more to the point, I think, for ourselves is an understanding of the importance of everyone—Buddhists and Christians and Jews and Hindus and secular people—so living that the lines are no longer drawn around churches or nationalities or religious traditions, but around the protection of the innocent, the victims. This will be a very difficult and long-term struggle.

I had it brought home to me in Israel that there is no religious group that can be relied upon, just because it's religious, to understand basic things about religion—the basic things about human life and conscience. We're in a bad time for everybody. There are very few models as to our way to be drawn upon in any community. There certainly are no states that one could look to and say, "A revolution has occurred here; they're acting better toward people." And the religions are going the way of the state; obsession with survival at any price. There is a terrible casuistry that trades off human bodies and looks on an abstract, future good as an excuse for present evil.

NHAT HANH: "Kill now and save later." That has been very true in the case of Vietnam too. Remember the time a certain village was destroyed. Someone said, "We had to destroy the village in order to save it."

BERRIGAN: "In order to save it."

NHAT HANH: And while bombing North Vietnam, Washington was talking about the possibility of giving aid to rebuild if North Vietnam accepted its terms.

BERRIGAN: Then, of course, the aid never came anyway. The promise was empty.

NHAT HANH: Returning to the Israeli professor—well, he also asked me about my loyalty to Vietnam as a nation and to Buddhism as a religion, because in our discussions I always put peace and human life above everything. So he asked, "What if Buddhism cannot survive in Vietnam? Will you accept that in order to have peace in Vietnam?" I said, "Yes. I think if Vietnam has real peace—cooperation between North and South—and if it can ban war for a long time, I would be ready to sacrifice Buddhism." He was very shocked. But I thought it was quite plain that if you have to choose between Buddhism and peace, then you must choose peace. Because if you choose Buddhism you sacrifice peace and Buddhism does not accept that. Furthermore, Buddhism is not a number of temples and organizations. Buddhism is in your heart. Even if you don't have any temple or any monks, you can still be a Buddhist in your heart and life.

The rabbi asked also, "How about your loyalty to Vietnam as a nation?" I think that question touched the very core of the problem of the Middle East. I said that if I had to choose between the survival of the Vietnamese people and the survival of Vietnam as a nation, I would choose the survival of the people. He said, "Well, we cannot agree on that. That is why we cannot agree on other things." So that was the end of the dialogue.

BERRIGAN: There are so many contradictions in such an attitude. I was thinking that, first of all, the only way Jews have survived is by keeping independent of institutions. They've always been able to preserve a certain spirit, a certain self-understanding, even while they were shunted into ghettoes and penalized in so many ways, even when attempts were made at exterminating them. But, also, I think that this very reproach—that of defending institutions against people—is the one they have leveled at the Catholics, and rightly so. Because during the Hitler regime, as it became clear afterward, when the Pope was confronted with the cost of defending and protecting the Jews, he hesitated. He thought of reprisals against Catholics; he thought of what Hitler could do to Catholic institutions—the schools, the seminaries, and churches.

It was this threat that kept him silent.

And now, it seems to me, this same idea—the institution is the prime meaning and symbol of the religion itself—is transferred to the state. It is said now that Israel is a sacred and secular reality which must be preserved at all costs, even at the cost of killing. They denounced the Christians for that attitude, and they have now adopted it themselves.

I know a Jewish woman in New York; she is devoted and brilliant. Her whole life has been devoted to the poor and suffering. She said one day, "I knew when Israel formed an army that is was all finished with Israel." She was speaking as a Jew who understood that there was something about being a Jew that is extinguished when you raise an army. She didn't begin from a religious point of view at all. But she realized that her people were unique because they had none of these weapons; they didn't function in the world that way. And that was a very deep truth, I thought.

The worst thing is to be in despair; there are many forms that that takes, you know. As Rabbi Heschel used to say, "The opposite of love is not violence; it is indifference." One sinks into quicksand and simply declares that there's nowhere to go, nothing to do; one washes one's hands of the human adventure.

NHAT HANH: When we were at supper, I described you as a bridge builder, a pilgrim. I told you about a Buddhist saint described in the *Lotus Sutra*, who did nothing but repair roads, build bridges so people could come together to live with each other. Well, what you have been doing—going around meeting people, listening, and building that kind of bridge—is a most important thing. And you told us about one sad experience of bridge building in the United States between the Jewish people and you. Say a few words about that so that we remember.

BERRIGAN: The difficulty at that point, I think, Nhat Hanh, was that there already existed a bridge of illusion. This can be the most dangerous kind of all—the one that is hardest to replace. People are constantly passing over this bridge, back and forth in their dreams and ideologies and obsessions and

fears; and they are being reinforced in all those things, import-
ing and exporting to one another. The bridge of illusion grows
stronger in such trade. But the bridge of illusion must be
brought down before a real bridge can be constructed over
which human beings can pass to and from reality—in either
direction—so that the Americans going to Israel may deepen
their sense of being Jews of a covenant, and the Jews coming
to America may enrich and contribute to that scene, instead
of trading in Phantom jets and fury and racism about Arabs
and the inevitability of violence. Across this true bridge one
would hope people could pass into a new way—a new land, a
new direction. Well, anyway, I had sensed ever since 1967 that
someday something had to be said; and when the war broke
out again, I gave this speech. Someone said it would be impossible to speak in a way that would not give offense in these
circumstances, and still tell the truth. So I managed to offend
everyone.

NHAT HANH: But the bridge of illusion has been shattered;
and only after that can any real bridge be built. The destruction
of illusion is a necessity.

BERRIGAN: I'm not at all sure whether or not that has happened. I hope something has happened, but I am sure I had a
great deal to learn in Israel also.

NHAT HANH: But we all see that what you said in 1973 has
led people to think again, to examine again their beliefs or their
habits, their way of thinking. That is a very positive act. We
cannot say when the fruit of such an act will come, because
there are things that need time in order to be set right. There
are things that the Buddha or Jesus said thousands of years
ago; they may begin only now to have an effect. You cannot
hastily say whether something is effective or not.

Something in you tells me that you're eager to try and prevent pessimism from prevailing. Indeed, it is not a good thing
to be a pessimist, to say that there's nothing beyond that. One
Bodhisattra, described in the *Lotus Sutra*, is a traveler who
does nothing except come to every person to say, "Well, I do
not dare to take you lightly; I know that you are a Buddha and
you have the capability of being a Buddha,"

BERRIGAN: I think this hope is also a kind of bridge of which the piers on both sides are reality rather than illusion. Hope expresses some kind of tension between where one's feet are and the goal which is still unattained. It's not that one is trying to beat somebody to the goal; it's really that one is trying to be faithful to an impetus which is already set in motion, an invitation, the invitation from the one at the end. That invitation expresses both the urgency of living where one is as fully and really and consciously as possible; and carrying that with him so that nothing is lost as the movement goes forward. I think there's a connection between modesty—being brought down to size—and hope, as opposed to immodesty and delusion.

NHAT HANH: We must explore more about other directions. There must be other ways.

BERRIGAN: In classrooms I doubt that things will go very far.

NHAT HANH: I agree. I have a friend who is a Vietnamese Catholic priest. He was very open in his way of thinking concerning Christianity and society and other religions. His students liked his ideas very much. But then he came to act—he got married. That reflected his freedom, his interpretation of Christianity—that and other things he did. Some of his students accepted him for a while. But when he married, the students revolted against him.

BERRIGAN: Why?

NHAT HANH: Why did they accept the things that were said and not the things that were done? Do they think that discussion is life, but that when you do something you then become unacceptable?

BERRIGAN: Bonhoeffer said that he spent a certain period of his life going around with a briefcase to religious conferences. He said that he still had to be converted to Christianity, even though he was a theologian. It was only later, when he began to suffer and be on trial and in prison, that he realized there was a deep difference between a theologian and a Christian. I think that that's a useful distinction because some people still exclude from Christianity anything but a science of Christianity. What they produce in their seminaries and classrooms is experts; but not necessarily Christians or, indeed, Jews or Buddhists. I doubt whether a Jew of the capacity of Abraham Heschel would come out of a classroom in Israel today, where the sufferings of the Palestinians would be taboo—never spoken of, you know.

Of course, the great cry in the liberal community in the West is that international conferences illustrate the universal nature of religion, its independence of the nation-state and its ability to speak across borders. But I think this becomes very questionable, in fact, because such theologians seldom if ever face their own nation-state. It's easier to fly over the nation-state; half the fun, as they say, is getting somewhere else. But it's difficult to face the state, especially when it's making war. One could spend one's life, in the middle of the Vietnam war, flying around the world outside the United States, talking about the universal character of Christianity as some theologians and scripture scholars did. But their Christianity never quite landed, so to speak.

It's very like the liberal American secularists who are running to China as they used to run to Cuba. After Cuba, they ran to North Vietnam. They spend their lives evading the United States, seeking a kind of abstract ideal state. When it became clear that Cuba had some dark sides too—many prisoners, persecution of poets and homosexuals—there was a great flurry in the dovecote. When the revelation of torture of American pilots came out of North Vietnam, there was again a great scandal. I'm sure that if visitors ever get beyond the tourist circuit in China, they will discover some dark things too; that will be another scandal. Meantime, while the ideal state is being pursued, like an El Dorado or a mirage, the real state is never being confronted in order to make of that real state something more decent. I've seen this so often, so often. And usually this pursuit of the foreign ideal is linked to a dread, a kind of existential dread and hatred of one's own country—an inability to see the goodness and possibilities and hope that lie within one's own people, so that one could work there very patiently for changes. It's a form of alienation, I think; some theologians share it.

But I was wondering if you would speak at more length about your recent exchanges in Ceylon. You had an exposure to religious people very different from my own. I think that would be very helpful.

NHAT HANH: That international conference opened my eyes a lot because in the last few years I have been living mostly with more open-minded people in religious circles. Because of that conference in Colombo, I was put back into the real thing. It was difficult, the most difficult religious meeting I have had in many, many years. I don't know how the organizers selected the participants. But most of the participants had degrees in religious studies: professors, experts. And they had a tendency to teach; but I don't think that they had much to teach in terms of religious experiences.

During the ten days of the conference, I intervened only three times. That means I took only about fifteen or twenty minutes in all in order to speak. But it's so hard to establish communication—real communication—between people. I told a few friends I was interested only in having a real meeting. The participants—I wanted to know what were their problems, their difficulties, and what people could do to support one another. But, well, that didn't succeed.

People discussed almost everything, including religious experiences. At one point, a professor of religion said, "I don't know what you mean by religious experience. I am a professor of religion; we have things we can think and speak of and teach on the conceptual level. I don't think that—except on the conceptual level—we have anything to exchange."

BERRIGAN: That's quite an admission. Did you pray together? Was there any attempt like that?

NHAT HANH: Oh, yes. At seven o'clock in the morning, the group came together to pray under the guidance of one of the participants. That continued for some time. Then afterwards, the prayers were discontinued because of something that happened during the conference.

The change came about in this way. We were supposed to have a session on the varieties of religious experience, Father Murray Roger was asked to lead the session. He came to me and said he wouldn't like to have a discussion, because discussion of religious experiences is somehow difficult. So, I proposed to him that we make the session into a program of contemplation, meditation, and poetry. We agreed; we set up a kind of interfaith program of meditation and invited a swami to join us. The three of us made the program, divided into three parts. The first part was a meditation on a pebble. The second part was a meditation on a flower; and the third was an act of encounter.

I led the meditation on the pebble. I gave a chant, an invitation, a meditation, that lasted about three minutes. I proposed that everybody practice complete relaxation during the chant, imagining themselves as the pebble which is dropped in a river, runs down through fresh water, and finally comes to its resting place. They would do that during the chant. When the chant ended, they would be completely recovered in the holiness of their being; not trapped, not attracted to the future or the past, completely aware of the marvel of their being. And three minutes, only three minutes, would be devoted to that period.

After that, I gave a poem about the reincarnation of a flower, in order to introduce another phase of the same meditation. Father Roger came with a basket of flowers and invited each participant to come and to pick one flower to meditate on, to receive the message of the flower. He offered the name of St. Francis, who came to an almond tree in the winter and asked the tree about God. Suddenly the tree blossomed. These flowers were like the flowers of the tree. They were to try to get a message and record it in not more than seven words.

BERRIGAN: Seven words only.

NHAT HANH: Yes. They collected the messages and gave them to me. I made a selection of a number of messages to go with the flowers, in order to make a bouquet. And I gave it to the swami, who then led the whole group to a hospital for crippled children nearby.

Most of us had not been in that hospital before, although it was nearby. When we arrived, we saw children who were mentally and physically crippled. We listened to the doctor in charge of these children; each theologian gave his flower to a child and comforted him. Then we went nearby, near the water, near the trees, for the swami to lead us in meditation.

But, a number of participants didn't follow through. They abandoned us halfway. They had the impression that a program had been imposed on them—a program not in their traditions. But they were especially disturbed that they could not object, because of the silence and meditation.

Six of them brought the matter to the plenary session and demanded a reexamination of what had happened. As a result, the morning prayers were cancelled. We just sat in silence. That was a step backward. Before that we had had prayer together, led by a representative of each religion. It's too bad, but that's what happened. Yet it turned out that the pebble and the flowers were what they remembered most.

Then there was the fruit salad. An Indian Christian, my friend Samartha, gave a very good speech of introduction to the conference; he stressed the need to go deeper into each tradition. He tried to relieve the fears of people, to emphasize that the conference would respect religious differences—because everybody was afraid of syncretism. He said, "We are not going to make fruit salad." And everybody seemed to like that idea.

So, the first intervention of mine was on fruit salad. I said, "People here don't seem to like fruit salad, but I think fruit salad is delicious." I told them of our sharing the Eucharist here on Holy Thursday and I said, "That was possible because of the sufferings we, Vietnamese and Americans, have shared during many, many years. The sufferings brought us together; our worship didn't come out of light discussions or anything like that."

Well, a few Buddhists were very shocked at the idea that I shared the Eucharist, and I think a number of Christians were also scandalized. But I can say that there were also those who had thought hard and who understood.

I made it very plain that religious life is *life* and that I could not imagine how someone could eat only one kind of fruit. Although there are kinds of fruit that one does not like, there are many kinds that one can appreciate. Besides, only authentic fruits can make fruit salad.

BERRIGAN: How was that received?

NHAT HANH: Well, I cannot say. There are many things that need time to be seen. I think many shocking things were said and the negative response does not mean that people didn't receive the shock. The shock is going to work in the future. You see, one of the six who opposed the pebble said to me at the end of the conference—in a sorrowful mood—"I have learned something. On the conceptual level, we cannot know much." See, that's only the beginning.

BERRIGAN: I think this kind of shock treatment is so important. We know so little of what we know. We have such a narrow conception of how the human soul operates. The most atrocious things can happen in public and make no difference to religious people, especially to religious experts. And yet, all religions are filled with such hope, such possibility. Ours is drenched with the idea of the corporate nature of suffering. We have Christ's words, "I am the vine, you are the branches." There must be a cutting of branches so that the vine may flourish. And then we have Paul's letters about the body—Christ's body which is one. If one member is suffering, if the hand is suffering, the whole body suffers. So many great texts and images to live by. And to think that they become the subject of textual inquiry! Like, what was the genuine text? Was there a comma here? The substance gets entirely lost, so that after a while a theologian cannot take a child in his arms.

I like what A. J. Muste said once, "What we need in the United States is a foreign policy for children." That seems to me a deep statement about a future which we should not merely throw on the shoulders of young people, saying, "They must be different. They must be better."

You were saying though that you also encountered some children in Ceylon.

NHAT HANH: It has been a long time since I saw children like that. Barefoot children in that background of Ceylon—a very green island with no sign of industrial pollution. The children were not children of slums; they were of the countryside: I saw them, and to me they formed a part of nature. I had a desire to come and embrace each of them. I stood on a beach alone, and children saw me and they just ran towards me. We didn't know each others' language, so I put my arms around their shoulders—six of them. We stood like that for a long time, and night came, but that was so pleasant. So, suddenly I remembered that maybe I could emit a sound, say something. I thought, Here it is, Ceylon, country of Buddhism. I may chant a Pali prayer and they might recognize it. So, I began a chant, "I take refuge in the Buddha." They recognized that and they continued the sutra. Four of them joined hands and chanted. The two others stood by, respectfully.

BERRIGAN: What does the sutra say?

NHAT HANH: Just a common prayer like the "Our Father." "I take refuge in the Buddha. I take refuge in the Dhamma. I take refuge in the Samgha."

To the two children who hadn't chanted, I motioned for them to join us. They smiled and joined their hands, and chanted, "I take refuge in Mother Maria." The music of this prayer did not differ much from the Buddhist one we had just chanted. And when I embraced each child, they were a little surprised, but I felt very much with them; they gave me a feeling of serenity and sanity. We were in harmony with nature, the land, the ocean.

BERRIGAN: One of the things that was so hard to bear in the Middle East was the fact that Israel declared, in effect, that the children of the Palestinians were worth nothing. And the Palestinians were, in effect, saying the same thing in their attacks on children. There's some deep despair about the future when one is willing to kill children too; it is as though there doesn't need to be any future. Who cares about the future? I don't know a more irreligious attitude, one more utterly bankrupt of any human content, than one which permits children to be destroyed.

NHAT HANH: Such leaders play on whatever is left of the concern of adults—of adults vis-à-vis children. People are shocked when they see a child tortured. The leaders know that, and they want to provoke that kind of revulsion. But by such acts, they destroy everything that is left of the concern of people.

When I learned of the Israeli reprisals, bombing children and women and those who were not responsible at all for terrorism, I remembered the story of a school teacher. He was very angered by one of his students who was constantly humming in class, disturbing the class. The teacher did not know who was humming, though the class was always disturbed by that noise. He complained to another teacher, and the other proposed that whenever there was humming like that, just punish one of them, no matter who it is—just punish one. Although you do an injustice to him, you have to punish someone. Next time you punish someone else, and so on. One day the humming will stop. He followed the advice and he succeeded.

BERRIGAN: It's called "upping the ante." You hope that through the shock waves you create, the terrorism you excite in the whole camp, you will strike at the leadership and make it less possible for them to go on. But among other considerations, even as a theory this thing does not work. Because the leadership never consulted the people anyway, before the first provocative act. You have a leadership on both sides which is acting in secret, without consultation except for a kind of terrorist ingroup, which, in Israel, would be drawn from the army and, in Lebanon, from the young commandos who are willing to go, take hostages, and die.

But I am sure no one sits with ordinary people, either in Israel or in the camps, and says, "This is what we propose; we want to do this. This is what will happen as a result of it. You will be bombed, for instance. Do you agree?" Nobody asks the people. They are never consulted about whether they wish to die. They just die. And so, the roots of the community are cut by a leadership which is utterly indifferent to the fate of the community, and which makes its decisions entirely on its own. A kind of hardnosed fatalism is the rule; some must die, some are expendable. We were at a loss for words to describe the spiritual degradation of such actions.

And yet, of course, the acts of terrorism and reprisal are very different. This is something that is seldom considered.

The technology on the Israeli side is an extension of American technology and is used no differently than the Americans used it in Vietnam. This is what is called "clean killing." It's killing which is laundered. Neither the people who commit the killing nor the people at home ever see the dead and wounded. The killing is rendered abstract; the sin is an abstract sin. There's no crime imputable. But, on the other hand, there is a great outcry when Palestinians strike in Israel because the blood is visible—the bodies of the children are visible to all. A double standard is always exercised when the technological world meets the world of immediate violence.

I said, in Israel, it was extraordinary that there was an outcry for blood after the killing of Israeli children, but that there was no word about the children the Israelis themselves had killed. One of the editors with whom we talked, who's a thoughtful, good man, said, "Don't you think all of us should address a letter to the American and European political left who have made a hero of Hawatmeh, who claimed responsibility for the attack on the children? Should we not say that this is utterly unacceptable?"

This appeared to me, in one sense, logical; I knew that, in America, elements of the left are so utterly out of contact with reality that they would elevate any violence into heroic activity. But I said, "I think we must pause. How can we address a letter to Americans and Europeans about the crimes of Hawatmeh, and say nothing about the crimes of Israeli reprisals?" A great silence followed this. It seemed that I had introduced a very complicated note into the discussion.

NHAT HANH: Just as children of today drink milk, eat vegetables, but don't know where these things come from. Various processes bring milk and vegetables and other kinds of food to the city. So, children are surprised when they see a cow or a chicken or a real cauliflower plant.

In the same way, leaders always have their machinery of propaganda behind them so that people don't see the bad side of violence. Technology helps them in that respect very much.

BERRIGAN: Also, one notices how intellectuals become the servants of violence. This was very striking to me. On both sides, the justification for what was happening was formulated by an intellectual group that surrounded the leaders. They offered a measure of historical truth in favor of their own side. Some of their insights were extremely valuable and correct. But the devastating point is that in their study of political science and history and the analogies they draw between nations, they give a nod to the violence of the leadership. They justify the actions of the leaders before the world—in their research, in their writings—and so cause the terrorism to continue in many ways. There's very real teamwork between the tactical, militarized leadership which decides the next act of war, and those who are verbalizing and justifying that act before the world.

Of course the same thing goes on everywhere. Johnson needed Rostow. Kennedy needed Schlesinger. Nixon needed Kissinger. And Palestinian leaders need several scholars whom we met, who are distinguished and who well know the history of Palestine and the other states.

It occurred to me, in fact, that neither side deserved the name *revolutionary*, because from the point of view of power already possessed or of power grasped at, the same tactics were going forward. The violent were in liaison with the justifiers of violence; the revolutionary appeal was no different in essence from the appeal of those in possession. They were saying, "We keep our power by violence," or "We gain power by violence." And the appeal, as far as I can understand it, is an insane appeal launched in an insane world. It's as though the inmates in *Marat Sade* are yelling through the bars at people who are behind other bars. There's no real difference between those in power and those who are seeking power.

The Palestinian leaders gave it away. They said, "No one heard of us until we did these things. We were nonexistent; then we attacked a school bus or hijacked an airplane or took hostages. Now the world hears from us. Now the world knows we exist. Otherwise we would have gone on forever in the camps, you see." And I said to myself, There's a terrifying truth here. I never heard of the Palestinaians until these things happened. But the appeal is insane; the world can hear only an insane call. So there is no breakthrough.

NHAT HANH: If those who seek power and those who are in power are not much different from each other, we may ask ourselves what conditions the behavior of the leadership? What part is played by free will, by strength? Why does everyone in power do very much the same thing?

When medical students and nurses are about to graduate, they think very much of helping the poor—those who have not enough money to go to fully-equipped hospitals, facilities like that. But after graduation, after a few years in ther careers, many of them begin to act like machines and pay no more attention to the poor and oppressed. The nurses become irritated at poor patients. The doctors become insensitive to the sufferings of the poor. It's very sad. To love is a difficult thing when the people try to cheat and trick you, to get the most out of you if you show compassion, goodwill; when they try to get the better of you, because you show concern. So, at one point you cannot love them any more, and you begin to treat them as you treat objects.

I think such things happen frequently. Our goodwill, our intentions, play one role; social conditions play another. And there are the political and economic systems. If we try to do things faithfully, in accord with our best instincts, we have to go against all of these forces.

If you are in power, they will try to bring you down. So, you make a compromise in order to be able to continue. You compromise to the point that you become like those whom you opposed before you came to power.

BERRIGAN: Making such a "revolution," one is almost like a person who is trying to pull himself out of quicksand. He tries to draw himself out of an awful suction of death, clean. Yet, nobody can come out clean. If you survive, you come into a new situation very much like the old—a smell, a filth of history, of human crimes. How can you stand on your feet again and say, "I am a new person, and I am now ready to begin functioning in a new way"? This is why I think there has never really been a revolution which transcended the past without submission before God, without faith.

I think that life always is ambiguous. This we accept, the human situation being murky and conditioned by the past.

But what we look for, as Camus says, is at least a world in which murder will not be legitimate. We don't look for a world in which murder will not occur; that seems unrealistic. But we don't want murder to be looked upon as virtuous and legitimate. Maybe that's a minimal definition of the kind of change we work for.

However, it seems to me that those who step out of the quicksand of bad history, by some heroic act of antigravity, still believe murder is legitimate. They call the killing of the "bad guys" a revolution. They ignore the fact that this is the most profound and bloody stereotype of history; everybody has always killed the bad guys. Nobody kills the good guys.

The Church is tainted in this way as well. The Church plays the same cards; it likes the taste of imperial power too. This is the most profound kind of betrayal I can think of. Terrible! Jews and Christians and Buddhists and all kinds of people who come from a good place, who come from revolutionary beginnings and are descended from heroes and saints. This can all be lost, you know. We can give it all up. And we do. Religion becomes another resource for the same old death-game, as we saw during the Vietnam war.

But I think maybe we're reduced to modest and small actions today, retaining some measure of sanity, some remembrance which will be viable. We must make the old stereotypes uncomfortable by asking distressing questions. I thought that that was the only thing we could do in the Middle East; perhaps it was the only thing you could do among theologians at the conference. You tried to formulate questions which were shocking and uncomfortable, which were a kind of access to the truth and to remembrance. There's not much else you can do.

Yet I don't think I have been courageous enough, lucid and visible before others, in a certain ethical position. We haven't been clear enough for our own people and for our own souls on these questions of violence. I'm humiliated to say that it has taken me so long to be willing to bear the suspicion or dislike of people whom I admire and stand with, and even to be unpopular on all sides. But now, at last, it looks as though I've gotten there!

3

Exile

BERRIGAN: I was wondering if today we could discuss the theme of exile. What does it mean to be an exile? Your community is made up of exiles and, due to all kinds of international complication and the continuing war, it looks as though this may go on for some time. I have some taste of this by being here with you. But it's also quite clear that my choices are larger—not merely that I can go home when I want to, but that I can go to other countries much more easily. Being a member of a superstate grants me international privileges that don't apply to you—and probably never will. But I have the impression that though much suffering is connected with exile, still, this is a fruitful and good time. I think of the work being done here for the suffering and helpless people, for prisoners, for the displaced. And I hope you too feel that your presence outside your country is of import to many.

NHAT HANH: One thing is that we were not prepared to live in a different culture and society. Also, we are absent from the people with whom we worked for a long time; we do not feel that we now share their countless difficulties. The hardest moment is when we learn of their being imprisoned or killed.

Here in the West, the society is so different. We never experienced this kind of life before—living in an apartment house where there are many families, but people are not interested in each other. It's quite different from being in a village where everybody knows everybody. Of course we have friends coming and going, but it's not the same. You see, in a

Vietnamese village we use terms like "second brother" or "sixth sister" or "second uncle" or "third aunt." That is due to our agricultural background. In the past, one family would set out to find land, would grow and occupy the land, and divide into many families. So wherever we go, we meet with members of the family.

Another difference is that in the Vietnamese language, the word "I" (*toi*) is quite different from the "I" in other languages. In our language, *toi* means "your servant"; there is no "I" as such. When you talk to someone, you establish a relationship. Sometimes, if the person you are talking to is a little older, you call him "big brother" and you refer to yourself as "smaller brother." Without that kind of relationship, it is not possible to talk. So one would say, "What does the big brother think of the weather today?"—something like that, instead of "you." When people come to the city, they address the people they meet on the street in the same way.

But everything seems to be different here; not only the culture, but the way of life. It's like being a fish out of water. Living abroad you feel somehow uneasy; you try to adapt. There are those who can adapt more easily, but for us it's not so easy. Our own safety if we should return home is not a problem to us, because our friends in Vietnam are facing danger all the time. Even the young workers in the village face danger all the time. So we don't think much of that. But I don't know why they don't let us go home and continue our work.

BERRIGAN: It seems to me that they've made a political judgment about religious people interfering, being troublesome to them. And they find it much better politically for you to be out of the country than in it. This is an old story; when religion is true to itself, it is embarrassing to the politicians. Then religion must either be silenced or exiled or brought around to another way of thinking.

NHAT HANH: In Vietnam, our community, the Unified Buddhist Church, operates without any legal sanction. Even the School of Social Service, which is doing the work of reconstruction, has no license to operate; the government doesn't want to grant one. And I think any meaningful activity that is going on is a kind of exile at home.

BERRIGAN: People always are conscious of that—that they operate illegally, without approval. It seems to me that by analogy, this is true everywhere. When good people are trying to do good work today, they are in this kind of trouble. They must be convinced of the value of the work, so they can go ahead with it. I don't know of anybody I respect who is not functioning under this kind of suspicion is not really pushed to the edge. I'm sure this is much worse, much more repressive in Saigon than it would be in New York; but we have had worse periods also.

I want to ask you, though, is there a Buddhist tradition that deals with being cast out, being exiled? We have this at the outset of the Bible; the exile from a garden is a very interesting beginning, the beginning almost of human history. Man and woman are exiled from their original innocence, from their original love of God and His love for them. So, all of human history after that, in a sense, is under a cloud; and particular periods of exile come, I think, to remind us of our situation before God: that we are sinners, that we are unworthy of Him.

Often exile becomes the occasion of a new understanding of how difficult it is to rebuild that innocence and that love, that community, which are often taken for granted in the normal, so-called normal, situation. For instance, in the States or in Saigon, if a religious person never resisted, never objected, never defended anyone, he could get along quite well; he wouldn't be an exile, he wouldn't be in trouble. But it seems to me that the quality and meaning of that life would be quite suspect.

NHAT HANH: In the Buddhist tradition, people used to speak of "enlightenment," as a kind of returning home. The three worlds—the world of form, of nonform, of desire—are not your homes. These are places where you wander around for many existences, alienated from your own nature. So enlightenment is the way to get back. And, they speak about efforts to go back—described in terms of the recovery of oneself, of one's integrity.

Practically, life in exile is often difficult not only in thinking, in feeling, but physically too. There are countries where you can stay only one or two weeks. Then they want you to go. And sometimes you don't know where to go. There are places where they confine you to one area. You have the feeling that this earth is monopolized by a few people and you are not allowed to be on it. Even when they allow you in one area one week or two weeks or two months, they are trying to push you on; you belong someplace else, not to this world.

BERRIGAN: That's a terrible injustice to human beings—to carve the world up and to declare who is eligible to exist and who isn't. Of course, it's another form of war—a war against human freedom and dignity.

NHAT HANH: They are most afraid of poor people and of people who have been active in their own counrty, you see. Before they grant you a visa, you must prove that you are not a poor person coming to their country to stay there, to seek a job; so they demand that you show a round trip ticket. Then they want to make sure that you have not been in trouble in your country. Did you raise your voice against injustice? If you have done something like that, they will give you only a visa to pass through—and out. Everywhere it's the same.

BERRIGAN: After a while one gets the impression that if you are really speaking up for humanity, you're unwelcome everywhere. I can remember being excluded from Japan, from England, many countries, just because I was raising certain questions, not ideologically, but about human beings—especially the question of prisoners, political prisoners. I think one has to have a very strong sense of himself, and a community at his side, in order to sustain all this

Anyway, such treatment is a reminder that it's foolish and retrogressive to accept a kind of citizenship that implies toleration, silence, and approval of crimes against the innocent, against the poor. These troubles at least shake one out of the idea that there's any regime that can be acceptable today, any regime in which one could exist in a human way and keep quiet, in order to get their stamp of approval on your life. Of course, it's a terrible thing to have to consider that there are so few countries that meet even minimal demands of justice or decency, but such seems to be the fact; which would seem to argue that practically everyone today should be either in exile or jail or in some kind of trouble. Right?

NHAT HANH: That's true.

BERRIGAN: This is painful to admit, especially for young people who have had the problem thrust at them quickly, and who are inheriting the problem without inheriting any solutions. The nation-state is becoming more and more violent and suspicious and repressive. Yet we have no clear alternative to all this, except to say No to it. But that doesn't create what we hope will come: a decent grouping of human beings.

NHAT HANH: Well, in principle we should be willing to live anyplace, because wherever we are, we have to continue to be ourselves, to do the things we want to do. But I was speaking about the kind of environment that one has grown used to, that one has roots in. You have made a commitment and feel that you belong to an area that's part of these actions and feelings. And because there are others whom you feel very close to, who are suffering there, you suffer too. Thinking of your people, your friends, your comrades who are being bombed, is very hard to bear.

I experienced that quite clearly during 1968, a period when the war was very intensive. They bombed, they shelled populated areas; there were people who died every day, people who were noncombatants. You have friends, co-workers, everywhere and you don't know whether they are dead or alive. There are many who die; you have to suffer the death of every one of them. When you know personally the human beings, those who have shared with you the difficulties, the problems, it is very hard. You want to believe they are alive, but fear that many may have died. I promised the head of the School of Youth for Social Service, Thay Thanh Van, that I would be away two weeks. He said, "Well, not more than three weeks." I said, "Yes." Now seven years have passed; he died two years ago.

BERRIGAN: How did he die?

NHAT HANH: He was killed by an American military truck while coming back from a village where he had visited some of our workers. I don't know why they drove so carelessly. They brought him into a nearby military hospital, but they didn't care for him, in any real way.

He was young; he certainly had to shoulder many sufferings. Workers, young people from the school—many had died before him. He felt responsible. One time the area surrounding the School of Youth for Social Service was bombarded and completely destroyed. I don't know how the school still stood. Only one bomb fell on the chicken farm, so nobody was killed. Eleven thousand refugees crowded into the campus of the school from the area surrounding. All around, the fighting continued, and many people believed that if the school was not bombed, it must have been through some special protection of the Buddha. So they came in and sat down. (Later I met people who came from the school, and I learned many, many things concerning that period.) People died on the campus, and babies were born there because there were thousands of refugees. They didn't know anything about the delivery of babies; they didn't learn that in school. But they had to do it.

One time the National Liberation Front came in during the night and set up antiaircraft guns. Thay Thanh Van was very worried. He said if they fired from the campus, the campus would be bombed. So he asked a young monk to go to the place where they were setting up the guns. He crawled there and tried to persuade them: "If you move outside the campus it would be much better. Otherwise, thousands of people will die." The monk was eloquent enough; they finally consented to move the guns. Thay Thanh Van did what his heart dictated. He wanted to have an exit by which they could evacuate the wounded refugees, but the campus was surrounded. So he went to the Saigon officer to negotiate with him. "If you will refrain from shooting, I will run to the NLF to negotiate so they will not shoot either." But officers from Saigon said, "How can you? Are you not afraid?" (Of course he was afraid of being shot by one side or the other.) But he said, "Will you consent, if the other side will?" They agreed. He ran back to the NLF and won their consent as well. Both sides let us move the wounded. I was not on campus at that time; and he kept the story secret for a long time.

The most moving story about the same monk was told me by a Japanese girl who worked as a volunteer in our school. She said that late one afternoon, about a month after that, the news spread throughout the campus that there would be bombing that night. The panic started—everyone began picking up things and running. Thay Thanh Van took up a microphone and was about to urge the people not to move, not to panic. But when he held the microphone he thought, but what if they really do come and bomb? He didn't know. So he slowly, slowly put the microphone down. For a man in his thirties, to make such a decision is so hard. A few years later he died.

Among the workers in the school there was a boy whose name was Ân; he specialized in helping the villagers raise chickens the modern way. He's no longer there—he died. I remember what he said to the peasants. He was asked by people of the village how much the workers of the school earned from the government. They worked so well; they must be paid a great deal. "Well," he said, "workers like us don't get anything from the government. We work on our own." "But why are you working so hard and not earning anything from the government?" So he said, "Well, we are performing merits." (There is a tradition that one comes to the Buddhist temple in order to acquire merits. It's a popular belief, trying to acquire these merits for your children to draw on in the future.) "In times like this when people suffer so much, the Bodhisattvas don't stay in the temple; they are out here. That's why we are not winning merits in the temple; we are winning them here." It was a kind of popular theology. Nobody taught him to say that; it just came from his own heart and understanding. That created a kind of immediate understanding, and afterwards the peasants accepted our workers.

Now, even if they give me a visa to go home, I will not meet these people. How many of them are no longer there? The girl who burned herself for peace; she did that only one year after I left. She wrote me a simple letter: "Tomorrow I go to burn myself for peace; please don't worry, peace will come soon." She wrote that in a very calm way. She was about to die but she still worried that we would worry that peace would not come soon.

BERRIGAN: How much of the experience of life today is a sense of being alienated, cut off, cast out, or put far from home! We were talking a bit before about Camus's *The Stranger*. Camus explored this theme quite brilliantly. An experience like yours is one way of sharing a universal experience today. Nobody who's conscious today is not sharing in some way the experience of exile. Even those who are in solid possession of power and money often show themselves most destructively alienated. They become enemies of community, enemies of compassion, enemies of human justice. So I console myself with the idea that exile, distance from such power, is a way of sharing other lives.

I think Merton was conscious of this. A superficial person might say, "Well, here's a man who never left the monastery. How could he feel alienated or exiled?" But he did. All the while he was there, he was alienated from the monastery. He felt that he had to be a protesting member of that community in order to bring any vitality to it. I remember discussing this with him. He thought this was an old part of the monastic tradition, being a kind of spiritual exile from the dead center. He said that in the Christian West we always had a tradition of the *vagus*, the wanderer, or the gyrovague, the person who has only a loose connection with a settled monastery. St. Benedict tried to end this by having the monks take a vow to stay put, a vow of stability. But, of course, that only takes care of the geography; it doesn't take care of the soul. Maybe there cannot be one place or even one community, from birth to death, which will satisfy the need of human beings to grow and move and become themselves.

NHAT HANH: I think that when you decide to do something in order to become yourself, and your thinking and your aspirations become one, you might find that you are quite alone. People will not understand; people will oppose you. A kind of loneliness, a real exile, settles in. You may be with your parents, with your friends, with your community, but you are in exile practically because of that situation.

BERRIGAN: Camus reduced this feeling to a quite trivial source in his novel *The Stranger*. The man doesn't commit some great crime against the state; he's not very interesting politically. He's in trouble because he refuses to weep at his mother's funeral. Even though he's killed a man, and that's the charge, what turns the judge and jury against him is a report that he went to a home where his mother had died, then went to the funeral; and he didn't weep. He lit a cigarette after the burial. This makes people absolutely furious. He dares to attack a convention, a polite way of coping or dealing; and so they decide that he must die. Camus says by implication: it's not that he killed somebody but that he just doesn't fit a human landscape; he doesn't want to do what people ordinarily do. So they lock him up and kill him.

I thought that was a sardonic way of saying two things: most of us are not very exciting people historically; and our crimes are usually not very serious. What turns people against others is not usually a big crime. The insight is true—people can put up with a great deal that doesn't immediately cross their plans, or insult their sensibilities.

NHAT HANH: Meursault went to the beach with a woman and after that went to see a movie; and these also are not acceptable acts when your mother has died. I think things like this happen all the time. There are those who don't want to go to college, get a degree, buy a car for the use of the family. If people don't want the things that all the other people have, they will be looked upon as outsiders. Why don't you do what everyone else does? But if you are determined to go your own way, to do just what you like or what you think is right, they think you are crazy. In such a case, you are a little bit in exile just because you don't act like the others.

BERRIGAN: I've been trying to figure out for a long time what possible circumstances would help me to, as they say, "fit in." I think this is the big anxiety in my order; I just don't seem to settle into any kind of regime. And, of course, in a sense they are right. On the other hand, what one is trying for these days is not a sort of arbitrary rebellion, without foundation or reason. One is trying to defend human life; and you can't do that by fitting into a regime. But at the same time, I think one has a responsibility to do one's best to help people understand. Perplexing questions come up. People say to me, "Where's your community?" I simply can't say, "Well, I live in such a street, and I have these groups and all this," because every year it changes. One year I'm in Canada, next year I'm in Europe; I'm here or there. And this way doesn't easily admit of acceptance.

All the while, one feels in exile. In many ways it would be satisfactory to try to have a more stable existence. I thought when I came out of jail that might be possible. But then I saw how things were going. And I knew that if anything they were worse than before. You simply couldn't close your eyes and decide that you were going to lead a professional life, or a so-called religious life. Of course, that decision meant trouble because people have the idea that after the sixties were over, the sixties became understandable. "It's okay that he did that; but that's over. That was an episode. Now he ought to be willing to recognize that the war is over, and come into a settled community and settle down." But nothing is understandable while it's going on—the sixties are only understandable when they're over, which makes most people into morticians —ready to bury the dead. But it costs something to say while killing is going on, "No one should die!" And the killing is still going on.

NHAT HANH: They are ready to recognize prophets once the prophets are dead.

BERRIGAN: Well, to recognize an occasion, once it's over, as having been prophetic or important—that's not so difficult. But meantime, we're not back there; we're here. So, what do we do now? It's very painful and difficult.

The reason I brought this up is that I believe what you and Phuong and Huong and the others are enduring here in Paris is one form of a universal metaphor. You're undergoing it in many ways: physically, spiritually. But look into the eyes of thoughtful people today and you see a sorrowful sense, something like your own; a sense of being kicked out, kicked out of paradise. They may even conclude that paradise doesn't exist any more. That doesn't make it any less painful. Then, of course, we have the false promises of technological paradise and the awful directions that human life can take today, through the media. Everything is promised: a return to homeland, to peace, to stability, to justice. And nothing is delivered. Better, they promise heaven and deliver hell.

NHAT HANH: The time when you feel least a stranger is when you return to yourself, even during your dreams, because when we dream I think we live more inside ourselves.

From time to time, I see in my dream a green hill—a hill of green grass where I spent time playing as a child, ten years old. That happened to be a place in northern Vietnam. And I have returned to that hill, that land, several times in dreams. Every time I leave, I leave things on that hill. I have grown trees here and there, and sometimes built something with the branches of the tree. Many dreams like that have been spaced in time. From time to time I have returned to that hill; and in the space between two dreams, the hill had grown. The hill is not a static image, it's growing like myself; and every time I come to the hill I see that's the place where I should be. And, each poem that I have written is in the form of a plant, a leaf, a flower.

Sometimes I meet friends in the form of a leaf or a plant or a tree. Each time I return I recognize these friends, and I see they have grown too. From time to time it has happened that something has stood in my way and I haven't been able to reach the hill. Very sadly I have returned, and each time like that I woke up with a feeling of sadness. Even in dreams you are not allowed to come back. I think the hill represents something like my homeland. And yet I know that homeland is not the hill where I played when I was ten. I know that if I were to go back and stand on that hill in northern Vietnam, I wouldn't say that it is the hill I have been dreaming of. One feels less a stranger when one returns to oneself, even in dreams.

4

Priests
and
Prisoners

NHAT HANH: Talking of prisoners reminds me of a story of Camus. A prisoner is to be executed in the morning. He is visited by a priest. The prisoner thinks of the priest as living like a dead man, and the prisoner knows he has to work out his own salvation. The chaplain cannot understand him.

BERRIGAN: The priest wants to "help him believe," he says.

NHAT HANH: Yes. The prisoner refuses not because he wants to refuse Christianity. He refuses "salvation" because he knows the priest who has come to see him understands neither himself nor the man he wants to save.

BERRIGAN: And in this he is quite right, it seems to me. That priest was only interested in some abstract declaration of faith. He came in bad faith, being in the employment of executioners; and, of course, a prisoner would be sensitive to that, if he has any self-respect at all.

NHAT HANH: It seems that the prisoner had a tiny window to look through, and he saw the sky. I think that kept him alive, not the priest.

BERRIGAN: Yes. Well, it's intolerable for a priest to lead people to the guillotine, and to have the same keys that the guards and the warden have so that he comes and goes freely. He opens a door and closes a door. When I came out of prison, I used to visit prisoners in Canada, and it always struck me

51

when I saw the chaplain take out his keys. Sometimes a chaplain would take you in to meet prisoners; and he would unlock the door. That's so simple a gesture. I said to myself, This man should not have those keys. Even if he doesn't want to be locked up with these prisoners, he shouldn't be able to lock *them* up. Do you know what I mean? He unlocks a door; he dramatizes his own freedom and the unfreedom of prisoners. A terrible thing to do!

But these chaplains grow so insensitive. It seems to me if one is going to be chaplain (and probably that's not a very good ambition), he should say, "I won't keep a single key. When you let me in there, you lock me in. And when I want to get out, you unlock me. I'm not going to touch those keys." That's a small point compared to preparing a man for execution. One should just scream aloud, "Stop the execution." But chaplains don't think this way, to say the least. I think there's no way of entering "professionally" the fate of prisoners unless one is willing to risk a great deal himself; and that of course can be done in many ways.

NHAT HANH: The image you just gave struck me—the chaplain who is the guardian of the keys. Maybe you should write a letter to all chaplains of prisons and give them that image; they might begin to think. One cannot hope to understand a prisoner if one cannot see oneself in that situation.

The prisoner in Camus's story—something happened and he became a prisoner. The problem of crime does not really exist for him; prison is only a chance for him to meditate on life and death. I doubt if he was really thinking of himself as someone who had committed a crime. But when the priest came in, he brought with him the point of view of the system that the prisoner was a criminal. How can we have communication established between the two?

BERRIGAN: The priest would have to become a prisoner—or something like it. He needs the essential modesty of a prisoner. Then he could test his own formulas of faith, which he's asking the prisoner to believe.

NAHT HANH: The priest may believe he is doing a great favor to the prisoner to bring him "faith." But put the priest in and lock him up in the prison!

BERRIGAN: Then see what happens to his faith. Maybe his faith is connected with the fact that he's going home at night!

It seems to me that especially in time of a war, such as the war in Vietnam, we try to understand whether a priest is not obliged to do something that gets him locked up too. In such a way, he throws away these keys and the privileges they signify, and becomes an anonymous prisoner with the others. And he's in there for some time. It seemed to Philip and myself that that made a great difference in the status of the priest; he became despised and even feared by those in power. But he also had friendship and brotherhood with the prisoners, and was able to minister to them in ways the chaplains never could.

The problem of how you minister to prisoners remains. It's not solved by saying that you come and go with a bunch of keys. A way must be found to prevent chaplains from taking the salary of the state and standing in the same relationship to prisoners as the guards. Such a chaplain is looking for the same benefits; he goes up the ladder the way the guards do in salary and in rank, and he retires with a pension, just as they do. This can't help but affect his relationship to the prisoners. In fact, Philip and I have never met a prison chaplain whom we could respect. Not one.

NHAT HANH: There was once a couple whose priest, a friend, was in prison, and they wanted to have their child baptized by that priest. So, they went in and asked him to organize the ceremony of baptism in prison. Could you tell me more about that?

BERRIGAN: Well, that was a tragicomedy. I only heard about it long after it happened; they make a practice of keeping such news from prisoners. Anyway, it appeared that a Vietnamese couple had a new baby and wanted this priest who was a prisoner (myself) to baptize the baby. But they were never able to get the message to me. So, all of this was settled over my head without anybody—the chaplain or anyone else—telling me of it. Later I learned the story and the chaplain's role in it. He was the kind of man who always tried to avoid issues. He wanted to have things settled elsewhere—by the bishop or by prison authorities—but never to take any positions himself. So, he asked the bishop about this request, with a recommendation that it be refused; then he could always say that a bishop decided it. The bishop said, "Well, okay. If you don't think it should happen, I will refuse." So that's the way he settled it.

Weeks later, I went to the chaplain one Sunday and said, "I understand you had an objection to my baptizing a child." He got very uneasy and angry, and said finally, "Well, it was settled by the bishop." And I said, "Yes, but I understand you gave a recommendation that the baptism should not occur." He finally confessed that that was true. I asked why. He got more angry, and more of the truth began to come out—his feelings about me and prison and everything. He finally blurted out, "Because a prison is no fit place to baptize a child!" I was astounded because I didn't realize that he felt so strongly. Then, I grew angry and said, "You're the type of priest who would have thought that the Mass should not be celebrated on Calvary. "So I walked away, and the whole episode stopped there.

NHAT HANH: Perhaps he thought, How many fine priests there are outside prison! Why didn't that couple go to one of them? Why did they want to have a prisoner baptize their child?

BERRIGAN: Sure. His attitude toward prisoners was, "You are in disgrace and rightly so; you're in prison. Therefore, you have no right to normal activity." If you were a priest it was a hundred times worse, because you were a scandal to the Christian community.

NHAT HANH: A prisoner is behind bars; he must have committed some kind of crime. Someone wearing that label has no spiritual, intellectual, moral capacity. He's a criminal.

BERRIGAN: He should be stripped of any right to exercise his duties; especially a priest. This is an ultimate disgrace for the Church, you know. I think the chaplain felt that he was disgraced even by having to speak to Phil and me, or minister to us. He was caught in a tremendous ambiguity because he also knew that we were honored for being in prison. So he didn't know quite what to do about all this.

NHAT HANH: In the case of Buddhist monks in Vietnam to-day, they have their heads shaved, and they wear brown, long robes. But once they enter prison, they are given the uniform that prisoners wear. And other prisoners have their hair cut like the monks. So, they cannot be distinguished as monks anymore. That is one of the reasons why the government has denied that there are monks in the prisons. Many of these monks have come to prison not through positive action, but just because they have refused to be drafted. In prison they find themselves with others, sharing the same conditions of prison life. The fact that 340 of them could organize a hunger strike, I think, is amazing. It took long, patient work because organizing a strike in prison is not an easy thing to do. But you find many ways of acting when you follow your conscience.

When Philip got out of prison I sent him a message, and I said that life out here is also a prison; the war is a prison. Everybody is caught in it. If you have done anything to displease the government, they put you in the army. And there you are a prisoner. If you refuse the army, you go to the other kind of prison—but they are both prisons.

BERRIGAN: We found also that a welter of distraction crept after one, just like a shadow, into jail. It became part of the apparatus of society against the convicted criminal, to keep him from becoming conscious. Just as it kept him from becoming conscious outside. All day and all night there was this underground of cheap magazines and photographs. The movies they chose for the prisoners were the most violent of all—either very low-grade sexual movies or violent movies. In other words, they had ways of keeping the prisoner disturbed and itchy and fantasizing—keeping him longing for what he could not have. They try to keep him off balance. We saw up close in prison the same assault on human modesty, human size, human understanding that we saw outside. In fact, in prison it was more pronounced.

One of the great tactics of the prison authorities is to awaken and make more violent the racism of the prisoners so that they will go at one another's throats. They must be kept in a state of turbulence and fear of one another that prevents them from realizing that they are all victimized by the same system— prison system, law and order system, or whatever. And in the worst prisons, we have evidence that the authorities awaken racism by false reports and rumors, and by supplying weapons and drugs. They keep these people absolutely insane about one another.

We decided that we had a greater obligation in prison to keep the discipline we had outside; and to bring some of the prisoners to agree that we would keep this stuff at a distance. We had our own program of reading and study and meditation and discussion. But, you see, the prison has a way of keeping the prisoners from becoming, as they love to say, "rehabil- itated"; that was the last thing they wanted.

If a prisoner became rehabilitated, he would be in resis- tance. He would say No to all this stuff, whether it was mass consumption or war or economic ambition or pornography. He would be in resistance, and so would become really trouble- some to the state. So, he had to be kept drowned in this filthy tide. Whereas, we thought *we* were really talking about re- habilitation.

NHAT HANH: Was there discussion about real change?

BERRIGAN: Yes. All the time. I think a number of prisoners became very different as a result. Some of them were able to see that their lives had been in agreement with an antihuman, violent, racist, consumptive, galloping way of life that was really a way of death; and so they became quite different.

NHAT HANH: Being eaten up by these things is not to live.

Many prisoners in our country have a deep understanding of why they are in prison; and so they are at ease there. It is like a balloon which rises until it reaches a point where it rises no more. Or like the pebble which sinks into the river until it reaches the bottom. Each thing in the universe has its own weight and will always find its own place. This understanding has led many people in Vietnam to take action that brought them to prison. But there they feel more at peace with them- selves. They have found the most suitable "place" to be in this situation of war.

5

Self-Immolation

BERRIGAN: I was wondering, could we discuss, even briefly, a question which is so vexing and mysterious for people—the question of self-immolation? As you know, we've had a number of these tragic events in the United States. And while it's been a source, I think, of inspiration and life to some, it's also been a great scandal. I can remember, one of the first of these events occurred in 1965. A young Catholic worker named Roger Laporte burned himself in front of the UN as a protest against the war. I was asked to speak at a service for him at the *Catholic Worker*. And I raised the question of whether or not this death could be called a suicide, because I felt that it shouldn't be. Suicide proceeds from despair and from the loss of hope, and I felt that this young person did not die in that spirit. So my sermon became a source of scandal, because the official line of the Church was that this was suicide and was not to be called anything else.

Consequently, I was in severe trouble as a result of that friendship and his death and that sermon. We had to deal with the same agony on successive occasions. Some of the people who died became known, and some did not. But I think such tragedies widened the conception of death as a gift of life in a way we had not known before in the West. We had never known an occasion where a person freely offered his life, except on the field of battle or to save another person. But the deliberate self-giving, a choice which didn't depend upon some immediate crisis but upon thoughtful revaluation of life—this was very new to us and was, indeed, an unprecedented gift.

NHAT HANH: I think, first, we should consider a few things. We should examine each particular case. I see in the act of self-immolation the willingness to take suffering on yourself, to make yourself suffer for the sake of purification, for the sake of communication. And in that respect, I think self-immolation by fire is not very different from fasting. Fasting is also to purify, to establish communication, to take suffering on yourself. And if you fast too long, you also die.

The Coconut Monk—you have heard of him—has many hundreds of disciples who have become conscientious objectors. When I asked him to write an article about Nhat Chi Mai, a woman who immolated herself, he said something like this, as if he were speaking to Mai: "Your uncle is also burning himself, in a slower way. I am burning myself with austerity, with active resistance against the war. I am doing exactly what you have done, but in a different way."

I think of Nhat Chi Mai and Thich Quang Duc—Vietnamese who immolated themselves. I knew both personally, and I think I understand the nature of their acts. I was a visitor in Thich Quang Duc's temple for many months. There were nights when I was busy writing. He would come to my room and just sit there and watch me, not saying anything for fear that he would interrupt me. I would continue, then stop and talk to him. Nhat Chi Mai loved life as much as Thich Quang Duc. She wanted to live. She was young, she had good friends, she loved life. Thich Quang Duc also. He was head of a community that looked upon him as a brother or father, someone you leaned on, relied on. Both have left very lucid poetry and letters. When you read them, you sense their desire to live. But they could not bear the sufferings of others. They wanted to do something or to be something for others.

As Phuong once put it, "If you want to buy something, you should pay something. And now you want to buy something very, very precious like the understanding of people. So you don't have anything more precious than your life. You pay by your own life. You try to exchange your life for understanding of peace, of brotherhood, and cooperation." So, they gave their lives in payment. But they still wanted to be alive. It was because of life that they acted, not because of death.

I would say that Jesus knew the things that were to happen to Him. Why didn't He try to avoid them? Why did He allow Himself to be caught in that situation—to be judged, to be crucified, to die? I think he did so because of others.

Nhat Chi Mai and Thich Quang Duc immolated themselves for others. Because of life. Because they saw their lives in the lives of others. And in a moment of perception of that deep, deep truth, they suddenly lost all fear and gave themselves. I wouldn't want to describe these acts as suicide or even as sacrifice. Maybe they didn't think of it as a sacrifice. Maybe they did. They may have thought of their act as a very natural thing to do, like breathing. The problem is to understand the situation and the context in which they acted.

BERRIGAN: I think when one gets beyond names and cultural differences, there's a great clue here to the life and death of Jesus. Especially since we're discussing this on Good Friday. (In fact, it's now 12:20 on Good Friday.) And one thinks of the proud and self-conscious statements of Jesus about His own death. He is anxious to free His action from any misunderstanding about His being a victim of circumstances or of evil. He is always asserting His self-possession—the deliberate nature of the death He is about to enter. So He says, "No one takes My life from Me, but I give My life freely." There are many occasions when they try to seize Him and He evades them. He says, "My hour has not yet come." In other words, He dies when He chooses to die. He doesn't die when they choose to take Him. And I think this is similar to the deaths we are trying to understand. The Son of man goes to His death freely, and His death is a gift to many, given in view of the lives of others and their possibilities. It is never a defeat or a base bargain or something exacted of Him against His will. I think the person who is capable of dying well is the one who is capable of living. The one who dies well is the one who gives his life with this free and full consciousness.

NHAT HANH: Nobody can persuade another to give his or her life in that way. Still I think we must try to understand those who have sacrificed themselves. We do not intend to say that self-immolation is good, or that it is bad. It is neither good nor bad. When you say something is good, you say that you *should* do that. But nobody can urge another to do such a thing. So such a discussion is not pursued in order to decide whether self-immolation is a good tactic in the nonviolent struggle or not. It is apart from all that. It is done to wake us up.

BERRIGAN: You know, once when I was underground, there was a very disturbing occurrence in the nieghborhood. A young boy about fourteen years old had been so brokenhearted by the war that he immolated himself one night in his own yard, in the front garden. He left a note to his family, went out, and immolated himself about three o'clock in the morning. His father came out to go to work, walked into the garden, and found the boy's body. This was another example of so many who went through that death alone— young people, especially, who couldn't bear the horror of the war and, as you say, not do something. They found themselves at their wit's end about what could be done and finally decided on this course. And this was a Catholic boy, as so many of these people were.

Another boy I knew immolated himself, lived for forty days, and finally died. He was very brilliant and religious. He decided on this all alone, as you said of the Vietnamese woman. All alone, not letting even his own family know.

I think in Christianity that something very great has been lost. Jesus' death, I think, in a very deep sense can be called a self-immolation. I mean that He went consciously to death, choosing that death for the sake of others, reasonably and thoughtfully. But the only way such a death continues in history as an example to others is in the military. Except for a few saints here and there who die for others; but that's very exceptional. In war, soldiers always go and die. And in many cases they die in religious wars. They die with the blessing: you will attain eternal life because you gave your life. But they die with weapons in their hands; they die at the hands of others with weapons. This seems to be so contrary to the example of Jesus, who refused to take up the sword.

So the Church loses any capacity to deal with the kind of death the Vietnam war brought home to us, in the case of a number of people in our country and, of course, in Vietnam, who chose this way. However, I think that these deaths were a nonviolent counterpart to those who killed and who died in armed violence. But would you say something about the circumstances under which your friends died?

NHAT HANH: Nhat Chi Mai, for instance, prepared everything for her immolation by herself—absolutely by herself. Her most intimate friends didn't know a thing about it. She spent a whole month with her parents in order to be a source of joy and pleasure. She was, as we say, honey and sweet rice for her parents. And after that, she came to visit our community. She wore a beautiful dress. We had never seen her in that dress before, and many thought that she was going to marry and that was why she had deserted the community for one month. She brought a banana cake that she had made at home. She divided it up and gave it to every one of us. And how she laughed! Many suspected that she was going to get married. She was so joyful. And then two days later they heard the news.

One remarkable thing is that when she knelt to die, she put in front of her a statue of the Virgin Mary and a statue of woman Bodhisattva, Quan Âm, the Buddhist saint of compassion. And she put a poem there: "Joining my hands, I kneel before Mother Mary and Bodhisattva Quan Âm. Please help me to realize fully my vow." In the situation of Vietnam, that meant very much, because unless the people of the two major religions in Vietnam—Buddhists and Catholics—cooperate, it will be very hard to alter the course of the war. She saw that.

BERRIGAN: It seems to me those gestures are a counterpart to the gestures of Jesus Himself. The joyful service of others at the point of death makes it apparent that this death is a fully human gesture—a human death, one that is taking everything into account. There are very few people who are given to die that way, that well, that consciously, that knowingly. Most people die fearfully or unhappily or grudgingly or in terror. But to die in such deep, deep joy and sense of oneself—that's a marvelous thing.

NHAT HANH: She also wrote poems, but nobody knew that until she died. Because she was shy, she didn't want to show off her poems. And so, they were surprised to see that most of the things she left behind were poems, and a few letters. She wrote letters to her family, to her father and mother, one letter to her coworkers, and a very brief letter to me. I was not there at the time. She wrote, "Tomorrow I will sacrifice myself for peace." And then she said, "I wish to contribute my part, and I ask you not to worry because very soon peace will come." Dying and yet trying to encourage others.

BERRIGAN: Yes. Yes. That's so. But this is typical, I think, of the resources of people like that. They have enough to give themselves in every direction.

NHAT HANH: When Thich Quang Duc and Nhat Chi Mai immolated themselves, they were in perfect control of themselves. They sat in the lotus position in full control of their bodies and, I believe, of their spirits. According to the people who were there, Thich Quang Duc sat very straight, very stable like a mountain, until he passed away. And Mai passed away very beautifully; she leaned forward in a position of worship in front of her two statues.

BERRIGAN: No cry, no sound?

NHAT HANH: No.

BERRIGAN: Silence? A great silence.

NHAT HANH: I know that during that period they had a very high degree of concentration. Once I went to a dentist and because I do not like anesthesia I asked him not to inject it when he pulled my tooth. All that time I looked at my hand with total concentration in order not to feel the pain. I believe that in the lotus position while they burned, they also had that kind of concentration, only in a greater, more intense degree. Because in my case it was only a tooth which gave pain; in theirs, it was the whole body.

BERRIGAN: What was the effect of such a death, offered by such an extraordinary woman?

NHAT HANH: One Catholic friend of mine, Father Lan, was so moved by her death that he undertook to publish her writings. And he was attacked by many Catholics.

BERRIGAN: Why were the Catholics angry?

NHAT HANH: Oh, a number of them thought of her death as a Communist trick—as propaganda. When you want to buy understanding, at the price of your life, you can buy it only to a certain degree.

BERRIGAN: Were the Catholics calling these deaths suicide too? As in the States?

NHAT HANH: Yes.

BERRIGAN: Therefore, beneath consideration?

NHAT HANH: Do you remember Madame Nhu? She spoke of the immolation as a barbecue.

BERRIGAN: You know, tonight, I see a clue that I didn't see before. It's very strange. I think it's because of our worship together and Holy Week and the very deep things in this community which I have gained some sense of. I see how these deaths would be so much better understood in the Buddhist community than in the Christian community. And this says something very deep about how our communities understand the offering of Jesus.

Why is it, for instance, that the Buddha's death was not at the hands of the violent, and the death of Jesus was? This is a very great difference, isn't it? Is it a matter merely of society and the culture of their time?

NHAT HANH: You might say that, but I also think that there is a basic similarity in their deaths. They both knew the time of their death had come and they were both completely prepared.

The Buddha was old and He knew that His time was coming. So He asked His beloved disciple to find a place between the two blooming trees and He made a last recommendation. Then He asked whether they had any questions before He went: "Have I forgotten to tell you anything?"

BERRIGAN: And then He died quietly?

NHAT HANH: One of the things He said was, "Light your own torch, carry your own light, and go." The Buddhist tradition speaks of the continuation of the lamp because of that: the torch of wisdom, the torch of light. When a Master transmits this, we call it the seal of spirit. If the disciple receives it, it is called the transmission of the lamp.

6

Government
and
Religion

BERRIGAN: It is part of the wisdom, I think, of the religious tradition always to be skeptical of what governments are doing. If their acts are done in secrecy, all one can do is to draw into that darkness the light of one's own nonviolence, plus the lessons of their past conduct. Mr. Kissinger did what he did in Southeast Asia; he's not going to be terribly different in the Middle East. One has to keep reminding oneself and other people that an exalted contempt for human life lies at the basis of diplomacy; and that one had better think of the unprotected and innocent, and be prepared for bad news when the leaders meet. And at the same time, one keeps one's own soul tranquil and modest, in order to be useful.

NHAT HANH: These governments always say that for their actions to be effective they must be kept secret. Somewhere their democratic claim goes wrong; it is no longer clear what kind of democracy they dream of. What can we do in response to their secrecy? If we accept the fact that some secrecy has to be kept in foreign affairs in order to be effective, then how do we find out what is going on? And if we find evidence of their wrongdoing, how can we make it known to the people? Because there is a whole machinery to protect the image they give. Any protest you offer, they describe as false, wrong, a distortion of the whole picture.

Concerning Vietnam, it is always like that. We have done everything we could to show the world what is really going on —even burned ourselves to awaken people to the truth. But some of the most drastic measures we adopted have been described as insanity. "See that man. He was crazy when he burned himself." Despite all the sacrifice, the killing still goes on behind the screens they set up. If we set up a factfinding team to find the truth, we would not be able to get in; there are all kinds of ways to prevent us. They also send factfinding missions in order to fabricate things that they want people to believe. If we report to the public, so do they.

BERRIGAN: I think one important aspect of this is the supposition that a well-informed public can change things. "Well-informed" usually involves one or another cliché about the role of the media—the press and television. We found, for instance, that in Israel there is a pretty decent press; yet the government for years did exactly what it wanted. The political effect of being well-informed in Israel is not much different than the political effect of being badly informed in Libya or Syria or Russia, where things are tightly controlled by the government and the propaganda is so overt. But, the idea that being informed leads to more humane decisions or more enlightened politics on the part of those in power, I think, is very questionable. Because the people can very easily, as in the United States, be lulled into a belief in "free press" and "free television." After all, for twelve years we saw on our screens what we were doing to the Vietnamese people. It's very questionable that that changed anything.

NHAT HANH: So even when there is "free press," a great problem remains.

BERRIGAN: Well, it's a problem which goes much deeper than the business of being what they call literate or informed. In fact, the impact of the media can quite possibly be in another direction. People can become so bewildered with the mass of information and news brought down on them that they're unable to more; they're paralyzed. So, the question of selecting, meditating, having some interior life of one's own in the midst of all this, becomes quite important. Especially in such times as these, to have a modest estimation of one's own life—that's a very important form of sanity. Just to keep the big world or the big lie at distance; in order to be available to a few people, in order to do one's work well.

The hunger for news eats up people, makes newsprint out of them. And there is, I think, another desperate form of immodesty—to become an image of a celebrity. Who was it who said that in twenty years we can think of a culture where everybody will be famous for fifteen minutes? And then it will be over! That seems very true. People get eaten up more and more quickly as the appetite grows for celebrities. You know, that kind of long view of the contemplative person who is doing patient, historical work gets lost. It is more and more difficult to keep one's balance. My solution has very often been simply to flee. It makes no sense to hang around and try to fight it; just turn off and get out. They very soon forget you if you're not available; and that's fine, that's really great.

NHAT HANH: To do serious work—that gets one in trouble very quickly. You know that in our movement many of the members, young monks and nuns, have been done away with, have disappeared. These things happen because the Buddhist community has been engaged in antigovernment activities, peace activities, opposing the dictatorship. But on the other hand as well, when others see that we oppose the Saigon government, they often think we support Hanoi or the NLF. This leads to the fear that we cooperate with the Communists in order to destroy anti-Communist elements in the country. Massacres have sometimes resulted from that.

The situation of the poor Catholic peasants, especially those who have migrated from the North, is most regrettable. They live in very bad conditions, just like the Buddhist peasants. Their lives are practically the same. But people tell them that we are dangerous and that we are cooperating with the Communists. So, they put us at odds with each other. There was a time when buses loaded with Catholic peasants came to Saigon, into the Buddhist elementary and high schools, in order to fight us—fight with whatever weapons they had in their hands, such as sticks and knives. They were told that these

Buddhists were cooperating with the Communists. Documents were circulated that created fear of the Buddhists. They announced, for instance, that on such a date and in such a place these Buddhist leaders met and discussed with Communists the strategy of this and that—all in order to awaken this fear. So the problem we encounter is very complex. Imagine a poor Buddhist peasant and a poor Catholic peasant opposing each other, fearing each other. They are not real enemies at all. They are both victims. They should be on the same side, but propaganda makes them stand on different sides. It is very difficult.

BERRIGAN: It sounds so much like the tactics they use everywhere, whether it's poor Palestinians and poor Israelis or, in Ireland, poor Protestants and poor Catholics.

NHAT HANH: Such conflicts are murderously difficult. Understanding and trust can be built only very slowly, step by step. Sometimes we fail and have to withdraw to find another way. But, fear and hatred are so easily sown. Especially in a situation like Vietnam where anyone can be suspected as a secret agent, CIA, or military intelligence.

BERRIGAN: I think that coping with the fear they try to inspire is one of the largest tasks of all. And helping people to live by other means than their fear, whether it's fear of one another, fear of the enemy, fear of the authorities, fear of prison, fear of disgrace, or fear of separation from families. In the last decade, it was a great project for us in communities to try to cope with this. Because the realities were never as gruesome as one's *fear* of the realities. It was that inflation of reality that the government was able to play on, until people could no longer recognize the difference between their fear of what might happen and what was actually happening.

NHAT HANH: Fear and anger are often used for political purposes. Anti-Communism has been very much used and fed, encouraging the fear that Communism will destroy freedom of worship. They stress that fear so the people will not see other aspects of the problem. Because when you consider Communism as the worst of evils, you can forget the other evils that are closer to you, that are on the anti-Communist side.

This has been a big problem for us.

BERRIGAN: That's a potent thing everywhere—awakening the fear of Communism. We had a saying, current in the fifties —"better dead than red"—which implies exactly what you're saying. Anything can be done, anything is morally justifiable, anything is ethically approved, as long as it's aimed at defeating Communism. So the anti-Communists commit the most atrocious crimes under the pretext of saving us from what they consider the worst crime of all. This becomes, of course, absolutely intolerable in the case of Christians, who are supposed to be able to cope with persecution, trials, jail, or any kind of human suffering, and still not despair. But it seems as though this spectre of Communism awakens the utmost despair, a kind of carte blanche to do anything in the name of anti-Communism. People really, deeply believe, under this awful barrage of propaganda, that Christianity cannot survive under Communism and that, practically speaking, you must first choose death. You choose death not only for yourself, you choose it for others; you kill in the name of anti-Communism, in the name of Christ.

NHAT HANH: There are many Catholics in Vietnam who have said, "The Thieu government is horrible. We hate it. But we have to support it because otherwise Communism will take over." They know that the government is evil and bad. But they use the theory of the lesser evil—evil, but still acceptable.

BERRIGAN: More acceptable after a while than any other possible evil. So anti-Communism, it seems to me, becomes the greatest possible evil, having created a spectre of an evil greater than itself, a spectre which has no substance, no real body, no existence. So it tries to match the spectre.

We had a famous play, when I was younger, about a conqueror who comes into a city. He is a huge, superhuman figure, and is preceded by enormous rumors of invincibility. He has conquered everywhere; this city is next. There is simply nothing to be done except to make peace with him; he is all prevailing. He comes closer and closer, and people begin to notice that he has no army; he is all alone. Yet they say that his army must be somewhere because, after all, he has conquered everywhere. Even if he comes alone, the army is going to follow him. So they surrender the city, give him the keys, bow down before him. And he stands there, and they wait and wait. Then slowly he raises his hand, lifts the visor of his helmet as though he is going to speak. Then you see that there is no head there! There is nothing there. Absolutely nothing. He is a huge goblin compounded of fear, dread, and cowardice. Outside their own fear, he has no existence.

NHAT HANH: An effective story!

BERRIGAN: And they gave the city away entirely. Coping with fear—that strikes me as a very important project as long as our lives last. Because the tactic of power politics, of the military, is to create fear so that people are paralyzed and cannot move, cannot change, cannot unite, cannot be truthful, cannot be in command of their own existence and their community. But if you break through this huge mirage, this myth, there is no one in the armor. You know?

A great man in Israel, the head of a civil rights group, said something to us I shall never forget. He is cut off from public influence there because he is so courageous. We had many conversations with this man whose courage shines out in the darkness of the war. When he said goodbye to us, he said, "Remember that whatever they do to us is much less than what we do to ourselves if we do not resist." I thought that was a wonderful summation of his whole life. This is what people don't think of: what we do to ourselves and our children and our communities when we give in.

NHAT HANH: In a situation where fear and hatred and anger prevail, we must still work effectively and we need, very much, the clarity to see, to be serene, to be ourselves first. And then, being so, we can reassure a few friends who are closer to us and can begin to think of something to do. But I notice that when confusion, suspicion, fear, go on like that, it's not very helpful just to keep on being busy. It does not help; often it just creates more confusion. So sometimes it's good to stop, to concentrate, and to become oneself again in order to restore a point of stability, before you start again.

BERRIGAN: This is connected, I think, with a deep act of

faith. Often when the sky falls in, your first impulse is to believe that things can never be the same again—that things are irretrievably ruined or that the powerful have finally won because they have you in their clutches, in their prisons.

But our experience has been that if one can achieve that calm you speak of, that self-possession, then many things happen independently of one's own powerlessness. I remember feeling this so often when I was captured and in jail, and then was indicted again at Harrisburg. You must get through those first weeks, days, hours, nights of black, black panic and despair. Then all kinds of things begin to occur, because there are many things that the government cannot stop. There are many human movements over which they have no control, many things friends can do, things that other people are drawn into, even the media. Such things alter the whole situation to the point where another very interesting struggle for peace follows.

That of course is not what they want at all. They find they've made a great mistake in indicting or capturing or trying you. But it takes a great deal of self-possession to allow things to happen, a great deal of patience to be able to ride with that tidal wave of fear which they stir up.

I think fear does two amazing things; maybe they are just aspects of one thing. First, it creates the impression that a person is facing a god, usually a god of war or god of violence; fear makes the adversary look superhuman. Secondly, it creates a new psyche in one's self—a very disrupted, distracted, terrorized person, the opposite of a stable, self-aware person. Two aspects, one fear. If one's soul is so enslaved as to bow to the god, one is already destroyed.

Again, it takes time to help people recognize the difference between their fear of a situation and the situation itself—which are two very different things.

The other great weapon they have, besides fear, is hatred. There are many authorities, especially in the prisons, who delight in awakening the hatred of prisoners because they know that this hatred distracts the prisoners from main issues. If they can siphon off a prisoner's energies into hatred of authorities, it's very much like fear, like racism. They have the prisoner at their mercy.

I remember one of the women who went to prison for war resistance—a nurse from Chicago. She destroyed draft records and was locked up in a very tough prison for months and months. She wrote that the hardest task she had in prison was to discipline her hatred—and she is a very loving person. But they do so much to bend your best energies in this direction. It's almost diabolical. A very clever tactic.

The one person in prison I had to fight against hating was a suave, sophisticated official. He was quite different from most. Someone said to me about him, "We can cope with the overly violent guard or the warden who quite clearly hates you. That you get used to." But this person was one who went in for a kind of torturing of prisoners. Not anything overt, anything he could be accused of, but a way of manipulating their sorrow, of withholding help, or of promising help and then never coming through. He sowed suspicion among prisoners, pretending to treat one with dignity. While he was in another corner, he was working against you. And he was a Catholic who pretended to deal with priests as a very respectful layman. One of the prisoners said, "Yes, I understand him. He actually wants you to hate him, to have you in his power, because you cannot do your work if you're consumed with hating him."

You can't do your work. I think this has implications for situations outside prison as well. I thing of the rivalries, the pettiness, that take over among people. It's a hatred that feeds on egoism, on the desire to be first, to be honored, to lord it over another—an inability to live with others in peace, to share goods, to share one's time, to be courteous and gentle and good with people. Someone said to me, in the worst days of the sixties, "We didn't really need Mr. Johnson around to disrupt us. We were very good at disrupting one another." Of course, we curtailed or harmed our own work by this mistreatment of others. That came out often. The time of the trials was also a heavy one; when there were many defendants it became difficult to stay together. There were many cross-

purposes and much tension. Those were great testing periods
for real love, I think.

NHAT HANH: Hatred seems to play a primary role in violent
revolution. I think that the leaders intend and try to make use
of hatred.

BERRIGAN: I agree with you. We've witnessed that in so
many countries recently—this business of awakening the
hatred of the people deliberately, through terrorism.

NHAT HANH: So that they can be ready to die, so that the
revolution may succeed.

BERRIGAN: You know, I was once speaking, I think it was in
Canada, to a group of students. They were showing a certain
contempt for nonviolence. Speaking of Angola and Mozam-
bique and the Palestinians, they were insisting that there are
occasions when you simply have to take up arms; it was the
kind of talk you hear every day. It's hard not to treat it with
contempt because it implies cowardice and distance from
human suffering. But I just sat there, and these people gave
their speeches. And then I said to myself, Maybe it's time to
speak more strongly. So I got up and said, very heatedly, that
we—my brother, my friends, and I—had done what we
thought was right. And if they thought that armed conflict was
the only way, they had two choices: one was to stay in Canada
and keep quiet; another was to go and join that struggle and
die and kill.

If they were sincere, they should either keep quiet in Canada, which is a very quiet country, or go to Angola and Mozam-
bique and take up a gun on behalf of oppressed people. But
you couldn't have both sides. Well, that made them more
angry than ever. But that was my way of trying to lay out a
fact: if you're going to recommend speedy death for other
people, you ought to go and taste it yourself; maybe it wouldn't
appear so attractive.

NHAT HANH: Once I gave a talk on Vietnam in the States.
One young man stood up and asked, "Why are you here? You
should be in Vietnam now—fighting against the enemy." I
said something like, "And what are you doing here? I thought
that the roots of the war were here, so I have come here."

I also remember listening one day to a seminar on South Africa and seeing some movies played of the atrocities and sufferings there. I remember being overwhelmed by sadness at one point. The members of the seminar asked me what I thought could be done. And I said I thought that nothing could be done. They seemed quite startled and asked why. I said, "Everyone is distressed by the films we've seen here, and everyone is discussing heatedly what action can be taken—whether nonviolent or violent. But tomorrow everyone will be preoccupied by his own life and cares, and his distress will vanish." If I had said we could do something, I might have left the people there at peace. But I felt that what was needed was a good shock.

BERRIGAN: We have a theory attributed to Luther which says that the Christian can kill another human being. He is allowed to do that as long as he has love in his heart while he does it. I think that is the most absurd paradox I ever heard of. It seems to me that it stretches the human soul beyond the breaking point—to say that a sane person can plunge a knife or fire a gun into another person's body and say to God at the same time, "I love him and I'm doing this for his good." You know? It shows that not only religious followers are sometimes insane, but also religious leaders.

NHAT HANH: And yet, that theory has lasted for quite a while! To be constantly active is the only thing that is considered meaningful by some people. Actions need energy. You get energy where? From dissatisfaction, from hatred. The more you hate, the more you become strong, much stronger than you were.

But when you are angry, you are not lucid enough for your action to make sense. Even in violent revolutionary doctrine, they talk of the calmness needed for making decisions. So, if you have to be calm in order to make a decision, you must guard against anger!

But those who do not make the decisions—they don't need calm. They need anger. So, you give them anger to fuel them. Then they will be ready to die or to kill, at your order.

From the religious point of view I believe that the only useful energy is compassion, love, concern. Compassion, love, and concern generate energies and action too; but this kind of energy can go together with calmness, serenity. The fact is that to have compassion, love, and concern for your fellow human beings, to bring these sentiments to birth in yourself or in someone else, is more difficult than to awaken anger. Anger is the easier way. It's like shouting your support for one side —easy—but it affects very little the situation.

BERRIGAN: Talking to leaders in the Arab countries, we heard, once more, a theory that one also always hears in revolutionary movements. They said to us that their movement is primarily one of education, of diplomacy, of teaching the people, learning from the people. They said their movement has nothing to do with violence as such. But then there is a necessary, subserving, military effort needed also. This is the theory. The armed struggle has to go on, or the other aspects of the movement don't flourish. But, they add, the armed struggle is never looked upon as primary. That is to say, people only kill when they absolutely are forced to this last-ditch measure. They, the leaders, like Che Guevara, see themselves as teachers and friends and brothers of the people. And the military is only resorted to because the other side is so violent.

This is the theory we heard. Then we came back to Israel; and a week later twenty children died, hostages. You're still supposed to accept the theory: the military is secondary; armed struggle is only ancillary. You're supposed to fit that theory into the new facts, even when the new facts are a horror. The revolutionaries have resorted to an act that every decent person abominates. Suddenly the whole theory is overturned, you see. The leadership *must* face the fact that in the eyes of the civilized world, they are uncivilized, militarized, violent, terroristic, and bloodthirsty to the point that the lives of children mean nothing to them.

One must say that the theory, which seems so beautiful on the face of it when the revolutionary leaders write and speak about it, differs mightily from their conduct. What happens in practically every instance is, if the struggle goes on for any length of time, the theory turns upside down. The military takes over. This may even go unrecognized by the leadership itself. They may still think of themselves as compassionate, loving, and thoughtful people, strategists of human change, architects of a human future. But all the while they're blind to the impact of their acts, the brutalized priorities which their group has accepted.

This also caused us great uneasiness about North Vietnam. The longer the struggle goes on, the more indistinct and blurred becomes every aspect of the revolution—except the military. That always becomes clearer.

NHAT HANH: There have been other ways of bringing change. After the government of Diem was overthrown, people began to explore all kinds of struggle. Some said the coup was not entirely nonviolent, because, at the end, the army intervened. But even the soldiers did not open fire, although they assassinated Diem and his brother after the coup had taken place.

There was much discussion, though I think it's very hard to draw conclusions. There was a lot of educational work; the people became aware of what was going on, how much we needed change, how unpopular the government had been, and how unwanted by the people. And all the things that we did were done without any prescribed doctrine, from the circulation of mimeographed documents to the self-burning of the Buddhist monks and nuns. In particular, the self-immolations were not planned by any movement at all. They were the decision of individuals.

There was no conscious ecumenical movement either. Christians and Buddhists, Catholics and Caodaïsts—they just struggled together. And we never said, "Now we have done all we can do. Now you, the army, you have to do the last thing." Members of the army worked side by side with nonarmy people.

There were people who described it as a holy struggle, because the intention was so pure. The struggle in 1966, 1967, and on up to the present has never been as pure as it was in 1963. Because, when we speak of a third force, of replacing the government, of all those things, there is always an intention of seizing or at least sharing power. During the 1963 struggle nobody thought of toppling the Diem government in order to come to power. But after that, in 1964, 1965, and1966, Buddhists, Catholics, Caodaïsts, thought of themselves, thought of their own power.

I certainly don't mean to say that the more we carry the struggle forward, the more we fall spiritually or morally. But I think the motive of the struggle determines almost everything. You see that people are suffering and you are suffering, and you want to change. No desire, no ambition, is involved. So, you come together easily! I have never seen that kind of spirit again, after the 1963 coup. We have done a lot to try to bring it back, but we haven't been able to.

BERRIGAN: So mysterious. And were you part of the whole struggle?

NHAT HANH: Yes, I participated. I had a hunger fast in New York; I helped bring the matter to the UN.

BERRIGAN: So, there was something then that cannot be just arbitrarily summoned again.

NHAT HANH: I think we have to meditate more on that. It was so beautiful.

BERRIGAN: The events you speak of seem such a shining exception to the way these things usually go, though. Whether we speak of Africa or the Middle East or Ireland, it seems to be more and more a stereotype of blood on both sides. Purity is progressively drowned in that blood, so that both sides are tainted by killing and more killing. Whether or not such movements can recover any pristine self-awareness of compassion is very difficult to say.

NHAT HANH: In that respect I think we have lost. I think the intensification of the Vietnam war makes it difficult to retain that kind of purity and simplicity. The Catholics saw the Buddhists struggling; they knew, without anybody telling them, that the Buddhists were struggling, were deeply suffering, that the Buddhists didn't have any ambition. But now there are Buddhist senators, Buddhist politicians. This is very different from 1963. There are Catholic senators, Caodaïst senators, religious-political groups, and things like that. And of course, the intervention by foreigners is more intense as time goes on.

BERRIGAN: Sure. It always poisons the atmosphere further. As we try to understand the direction of these struggles, which, I think, is a direction downward, the attitude of one who wants a different direction must be a very thoughtful one. One finds oneself more and more excluded from public life for reasons of conscience. It seems to me that one cannot take part in these death games, no matter what their declared intention. Or perhaps one must find a *different way* to take part in public responsibility. Maybe that's a better way of putting it; I don't think that one can just wash his hands. But, it certainly is a different part. There are so many things that we have to stand aside from in the States, just because they partake more and more of this death method. And then, if one chooses another way, as you've often said, he finds himself more and more alone.

NHAT HANH: We continue to learn from our failure and success. Since the success of 1963, at least one million people have come and said, "We need a Buddhist political party. If you are not organized politically, you cannot succeed." Everyone has been saying that. There are politicians now who want the support of the Buddhist bloc. They call themselves Buddhist politicians and they compete with Christian politicians. The trust we had in each other in 1963 has disappeared.

Then, after the signing of the Paris accords, we made another effort. We said, "Now let us disassociate ourselves from any political party, including people who call themselves Buddhist politicians. We don't need a political party. Let's act as a religious community only, doing work of reconciliation and healing." I was one of the members who strongly advocated that. Because I could not go to Vietnam, I met with colleagues in Asia and we helped make that decision: to describe ourselves as a nonpolitical religious movement, to avoid giving the impression that we were going to support a Buddhist government against a Caholic government or a Communist government or Caodaïst government.

After we had adopted that attitude, we began to be attacked by politicians—Buddhist politicians as well—because of our determination to return to a purely religious stance.

But we made the right decision. Why does the Buddhist church need a "Bureau of Liaison of Buddhist Senators and Congressmen"?

We monks know that our strength is not as a political group; our strength is as a religious group. We monks have seen that in the past we have been deceived by politicians, made use of by politicians. We want to get back to our own ground, struggle on religious ground only, and restore the purity we had in 1963.

BERRIGAN: Your position seems to me close to those in the United States who say that priests do not belong in the Congress. We believe it is regrettable when a priest is involved in making bargains with his voters and constituents and fellow congressmen, and so has no opportunity, energy, or enthusiasm for announcing the gospel. He incurs debts to the people who elected him. They want something from him. He has to give and take with other congressmen. After a while it becomes very unclear why he was ordained a priest at all or how his political life is different from anybody else's.

NHAT HANH: The vocation of a priest is quite different from the vocation of a politician.

BERRIGAN: I think so. I like the saying: "Whenever the prophet sits at the king's table, both are corrupted." Both —the king is corrupted and the priest is corrupted. The priest doesn't belong there. If he belongs anywhere in the palace precincts, he belongs in the king's dungeons. He doesn't belong at his table. But the current argument is that we're not talking about kings anymore; we're talking about a democracy. Nobody owes debts to a king. Well, I say you owe debts to the democrats. You owe debts to the voters. The new arrangement doesn't change the debts; it just spreads them further.

What is the feeling about this in the Buddhist community? Is there any parallel opinion and belief among Buddhists?

NHAT HANH: In our tradition there was no free political competition. When the king was a Buddhist, he could be a good Buddhist or just a Buddhist in name. If he was a good Buddhist, a monk could come and help him, and convince him to take the vow of the Bodhisattva. Then he would keep the discipline and vow, trying to preserve peace, respect life, and become a protector of the law. There are gods called protectors of the dharma; the king could be one of the protectors because he had that power, that gift of governing.

In our tradition, when the country suffered, it was believed that it was the faults of the ruling emperor.

BERRIGAN: Really?

NHAT HANH: It was believed that when disaster occurred, it was because his virtue and his heart were not pure enough, his motivation was not pure enough. So bad things happened. Then he had to issue a declaration. Throughout the Lê Dynasty, we have many records of the confessions of the emperors. He would say, "I, emperor of Dai Viet, confess that I have not done my best and my heart is not pure enough. I confess before the people, before Heaven, before the Earth. I will do better." Then he would sleep on a mat, not on his royal bed anymore. He would eat vegetarian meals and say, "I do this in repentance, purifying my heart." Sometimes, in spite of everything, the catastrophe continued [Laughter].

BERRIGAN: But, still, that's a profound understanding of things. Somehow the sins of those in charge flow over into nature, and nature revolts.

NHAT HANH: Not all the emperors who did that believed in that. However, because the people believed in that, an emperor had to confess his—

BERRIGAN: Sins.

NHAT HANH: So sin was a political reality too.

In Vietnam today, most people would not consider a monk as a serious monk if he ran for public office.

I think the desire for a Buddhist political party shows the naiveté of some of the monks. In fact, we have nothing we can really call Buddhist politicians. These politicians are not really practicing Buddhists, although they describe themselves as Buddhists. They say, "Well, if you don't have Buddhists to protect you in the senate or in the lower house, then you may be vulnerable." They always play on the fear of those who want to protect the dharma, to preserve Buddhism. They were able to convince a number of monks in the provinces to talk about electing Buddhist candidates, just as we have progovernment candidates or Catholic candidates. As a result, people voted for so-called Buddhist candidates. The other reason they received votes is that if one is called a Buddhist, he is expected more or less to oppose the government. So if you are offered two candidates—one progovernment and one Buddhist —even if you are not sure that he is Buddhist, it's safer to vote for him.

The fact is that most of the senators and congressmen who were elected as Buddhist candidates never joined our struggle. There were a few who associated themselves with resettling refugees, a few who came to the Buddhist pagoda in time of demonstrations. But the majority did little or nothing. They just used the Buddhist label.

BERRIGAN: That seems to be true everywhere. And that's the end of any real struggle, once such people get elected.

NHAT HANH: So we decided that it would be more helpful to stay away from the political scene. We would distinguish between our struggle and the political struggle. Of course, one must know the political situation in order to act wisely.

BERRIGAN: Tell me though, has there in the past been a serious effort on the part of monks to assume political office themselves?

NHAT HANH: This happened in 1945, after the revolution, when we got independence. There was a Buddhist monk who ran for the National Assembly—Thich Mât Thê. But that is exceptional. People voted for him as a monk because at that time the Buddhists were openly participating in national political affairs. After the French domination was ended, a Vietnamese government came to power and the government appealed to everyone to participate: Christians, Buddhists, and others. So we set up the Patriot Buddhist Association, the Patriot Christian Association, and the Patriot Children's Association. Everything "patriotic." The government wanted us to be present at any demonstration they organized. Catholic priests and Buddhist monks should be present! It was a revolutionary period, and demonstrations were organized by the government in order to educate the people. In that atmosphere, a monk—Thich Mât Thê, the author of a book on the history of Buddhism in Vietnam—became prominent. He had been active in the movement of reform of Buddhism, became the candidate, and was the only monk who ran and was elected as a member of the assembly. There, he struggled to protect Buddhism. But since that day, we have learned a lot. Now if a Buddhist monk becomes a candidate for elections, people do no take it seriously.

BERRIGAN: Is he disciplined by the Church if he runs for office?

NHAT HANH: No, he is free to do that. But he is not encouraged. In the Buddhist church, the sentiment of the people is more important than the statements of the hierarchy.

BERRIGAN: I see. Well, it seems to me, it's a sign of the decline of the whole religious community that priests take on the role of politicians. It's a loss of a clear-cut sense of their priesthood. If you're Quakers, that's something different. Let Quakers be either indifferent or passionate about politics. But if you're going to have an ordained priesthood, it seems to me, you're setting up clear lines for those who become priests, as well as for the church which accepts them. And apart from any doctrine. I think, such ventures have a bad history. Every time priests have played politics, there's been a deleterious effect upon the priesthood, the community, and the civil life as well.

NHAT HANH: Once drawn into politics you are caught. A monk is much listened to by the people. In a time of election people ask his advice, and his voice carries weight. But suppose he runs for office; he loses the respect people have for him. As a monk he speaks out of his wisdom, his spirituality. But when he runs for office, even if he is able to retain that spirituality and wisdom, people cannot help thinking that he has ambition. That changes the situation, you see.

BERRIGAN: For instance, it would be impossible for a political priest to go into the Middle East as we just did and to be received by both sides, by people who are willing to talk because they know one represents no special interest.

NHAT HANH: Yes. If you do not hold office, you have a different kind of strength, I think.

BERRIGAN: But I feel badly that the Jesuits only lately got uncomfortable with McLaughlin in the White House. My feeling is that in his case, religion followed the culture instead of giving leadership to the culture. If we were giving leadership, that priest would have been confronted years ago when he was defending Nixon's war crimes and war policy. That was never mentioned. The priest was in trouble because Nixon was in trouble; only because of domestic crimes. But the terrible question of the relationship of religion to the Vietnam war, the justifying of bombings—none of this ever became an embarrassment. This purported minister of the gospel went around the world justifying the war, smoothing the way for Nixon's travels. And superiors never said a word. But a really prophetic community would have said, three or four years before "Don't even take such a job. It will turn out badly." But nothing was said; so we face the same judgment of God that the country faces on the war. Through silence we abetted crimes.

NHAT HANH: There is great need for an ethics of behavior regarding the religious community vis-à-vis the government. A church usually seeks comfortable conditions for its existence. That's the normal tendency. To be on good terms with a government is a way of strengthening the church position. That is why religious communities gradually lose their integrity and are linked to the machinery that causes oppression and injustice. So, somehow both a religious community as well as a religious individual have to oppose the existing government.

I have the impression that in order to be ourselves we should oppose *any* government in power, we should be a kind of permanent opposition. But there may be other aspects. If, for example, the government does a few things that we think are going in the direction of justice, we can show our appreciation of that. We can show that we are not antigovernment but that we just want the government to do better.

BERRIGAN: A hundred times better. But what's the basis for opposition to the government in Buddhist tradition? For instance, we have a strong tradition, through our scriptures and through Jesus, of opposition to the state. Though we haven't been faithful to it, it's still deep in the tradition. Is that opposition also in the Buddhist scripture and the teachings of the Buddha—opposition to the state as part of Buddhism?

NHAT HANH: Well, in the Buddhist discipline, the monks are recommended not to approach people in power. That means governments. You only come to them on invitation, to teach the dharma. I think that reticence has even been exaggerated in the behavior of monks. There has developed a kind of arrogance vis-à-vis power. The monks have a complex that if they go to the people who have power, like emperors and statesmen, they will be despised by the people, the laymen.

But it's clear in Buddhist scriptures that monks should not mingle in political affairs. This is clear. During the ninth, tenth, and eleventh centuries, because the monks were the best educated people in the country, they had to help. They took care of many things, including education. They even had to receive ambassadors, because it happened that sometimes the emperor was not very well educated. But they didn't hold any office. And after advising the king, they would withdraw to their temples and live as monks again.

7

Economics
and
Religion

BERRIGAN: I was hoping we could say something about an aspect of church life that strikes me as being a key to our difficulties in the States. I mean the attitude of the church toward money. It affects everything—a kind of gentlemen's agreement, never spoken of. It was our investments that were keeping us, in many cases, from telling the truth about the war or giving witness to peaceableness during the war. We simply couldn't do it because we were bound to property and possessions. In the church hierarchy, there is practically no one who admits the connection between our consciences and our investments. It seems to me that we will never really become a church until this is faced.

NHAT HANH: The church reflects the society in which it exists.

BERRIGAN: But still the Buddhist church has had the opportunity to be rich or at least less poor than it is. In your society up to now, you have chosen to remain poor; and in that way you have been different from the society.

NHAT HANH: In Vietnam we have capitalists, but the poor people are the majority. The church is created by poor people. They build pagodas by themselves; they support the work of reconstruction. But there are also friends who try to influence us that we should have a stronger financial base to be more effective. There are a few monks who are persuaded of the rightness of this. But they have not prevailed. We know that our strength lies in the fact that we have no investments. Now throughout the country the small Buddhist communities have met to become self-supporting. This means just small enterprises—a cooperation for production of soy sauce, a printing house, a soap factory—only small artisan enterprises. That is why unity can exist among the more liberal monks and the more conservative ones, because behind each monk, each community, there are no big institutions. There is nothing to intimidate us. If one group in the monastery proves to be quite conservative in their thinking, it's not because they're bound to vested interests, but because they're just misinformed. We see the possibility of changing their viewpoint.

For instance, when *Lotus in a Sea of Fire* was circulated in Vietnam, some of the monks said it was pro-Communist. They said so, not because they read the book, but because they heard that the author of that book was a leftist. But our friends and fellow monks approved that book. They continued to circulate it among the monks and people, and the book became widely accepted. People asked one monk who had objected strongly if he had read that book and told him it was very good. So he began to read it. Finally he said, "Bring me fifty copies of this book." Now he has copies with him, and every time a neighbor comes to visit him, he asks, "Have you read this book? It's very good."

Whenever I feel that I cannot persuade the Buddhist leadership to take a certain action, I don't leave it at that. I just go off awhile and mix with people and work on the issue until the issue is recognized by the people as important. Then, when the opinion of the people is formed, I go back to the Buddhist leadership. They will follow. It's like a river: the water ahead cannot draw the water behind with it; but the water behind pushes the water ahead.

BERRIGAN: So they form together one current.

In the States, a source of agony for us has been the immobility and neutrality of the churches facing the tragedy of the last decade. We are convinced that financial interests are at the heart of it. We sense a freedom of conscience in the Buddhist church—the fact that the Buddhists are able to see a moral issue and to follow through on it, even to death itself. Whereas in our country it is so rare to come upon this sense of things.

I don't want to be oversimple about it, with pseudo-Marxist analysis. Everything in human life is not reducible to economics. I think it's more complex than that. But still one has to recognize, in a way that is not recognized by those in authority, that their judgments are influenced, even though they would deny it, by their holdings, and by their responsibilities to other shareholders or those who are supporting the churches with large sums of money. The Church represents special interests back somewhere.

We try to cut the knot in two ways: first, to understand our own churches better; and second, to understand the direction we should go. We've always tried to remain independent of money in our own communities, in groups, antiwar groups. But tell me, does the Buddhist tradition require, as our tradition does, that the monks take a vow of poverty? Or is that just presupposed?

NHAT HANH: A sangha is a community that consists of at least four monks. Basic laws of community life are set up for sangha. One of them is sharing the material things of the community. Each monk has only his three robes, his one bowl, his mat; that is his property. The other things belong to the monastery, and are used according to need.

BERRIGAN: When you founded the School of Youth for Social Service, how did you finance that?

NHAT HANH: Well, we did not have any money. I proposed to the An Quang pagoda that they set up a university that would adopt a quite different way of education than the university in Saigon. The monks asked how I thought I was going to get the money and facilities to build a university. I said, "Well, if only you agree I will find a way to do it." So they agreed. That is how I started. I began meeting with friends: professors in Saigon University, writers, and others. I told them, "I want to set up a university." They said, "All right, we will teach without pay because we are all employed elsewhere."

Then we discussed how to advance this work. I spent about one week going to persuade the abbots of a number of pagodas. We borrowed rooms in three pagodas for classrooms, a library, and offices. The teachers volunteered to draw up a program that combined the best elements of education we know of in our country and elsewhere. We tried to spend as little as we could. For the first time in Vietnam we had a school for social services as one school in a university. We asked the students to pay a small tuition if they could, because we didn't have any money. In universities in Vietnam people don't have to pay tuition. For the School of Youth for Social Services we also asked a nuns' temple to give us a place for an auditorium and two offices; and they gave us chairs, tables, desks—things like that. Then we organized in groups of three, and we went from house to house with a letter which I signed: "We need your help in order to set up a school of social services." We succeeded.

If you do kind things with a pure heart, I think you will get support. Money is not the most important thing. Also, I and other friends established a publishing house which is now one of the most important publishing houses in South Vietnam. The name of the publishing house "La Bôi" means "Palm Leaves." (In the old time, they wrote the scriptures on palm leaves.) We began with my borrowing forty thousand piasters. At that time, one dollar was about one hundred piasters; we had only forty thousand piasters. I gave them two manuscripts of mine, and I accepted no royalties. Now they have published the books of many hundreds of people.

BERRIGAN: Do you agree then that the independence of the church from material possessions and investments has been a source of its resistance, of its strength?

NHAT HANH: Yes. I think if we do not rely on the people we get nowhere—but it depends on what kind of people you rely on. If you rely on rich people, then that's the end. But the monks rely on street merchants—people who sell fish and vegetables in the markets—and pedicab drivers. They are the most faithful people in the society. You can trust them; they stick to the struggle. Not like the intellectuals. I don't believe in the intellectuals very much. In the demonstrations, we have to count on these poor people. It is they who organize, and not the intellectuals. When Nhat Chi Mai burned herself, the police came and surrounded the temple, and not many intellectuals dared to come. But the merchants from different markets came by the hundreds. Someone just went to each market and told one contact there. Five, ten minutes later, hundreds of people from that market rushed to the temple. Nothing was permitted to appear in the press the next morning, even when they prepared the funeral of Nhat Chi Mai. Newspapers could not announce the time and place. But thousands of people came to accompany her body to its resting place.

If you have too much, you don't rely on the support of the poor people. You might become arrogant or be cut off from your true resources.

BERRIGAN: What do Buddhists do about the temptation to become wealthy? Obviously you have wealthy Buddhists. Don't they come and offer gifts and money and all kinds of opportunity to enrich the church?

NHAT HANH: Well, in the past there were a number of people who gave the Buddhists land so that the temples would have means of self-support. The monks worked the land. Sometimes there were people who had no children and wanted to arrange for the yearly prayer service commemorating the day of their death. If they did not have any children, there would be no one to do that when the day came. They would give their land to the Buddhist temple, and the monks would arrange that a service be held for them on those days.

Now there are not many rich Buddhists; if there are, they don't give much to the temples. Sometimes they believe that if they contribute money to build a pagoda or for a statue of Buddha, they will acquire merits. Of course that is a kind of selfish motivation. I know a few rich people who gave money to the School of Youth for Social Service. But they had to do it secretly to prevent the government from knowing.

Ninety percent of the support is from the poor, without whom you cannot survive. It's very moving to see that they are poor like that, and yet contribute. The vendors, merchants, a lady who sells rice cake at the market—she has many contributions to make. She gives a dispensary a few piasters each month; she has to give ten piasters to an orphanage. There are many small merchants like that who support different kinds of work. Without them we cannot go on.

BERRIGAN: Could you say a bit more about your publishing house—its financing?

NHAT HANH: It's funny. The La Bôi Publishing House has no boss. I was a kind of founder. I went to one district and asked a woman to lend us forty thousand piasters. Then I asked a young monk to be manager. I suggested, "In order to have some money to travel and to buy food, you should take something like three thousand piasters a month. You need two assistants; give them each two thousand piasters a month." He agreed. I never looked into the records. But anyone, although he had no role in the company, could ask to look into the records. Students and others came from time to time to help arrange and sell books.

Once I got a letter from a student saying, "You don't think three thousand piasters is enough for a manager of a publishing house, do you? You must give him six thousand." So, I went to the monk. I said, "If you think we have the resources to pay six thousand, please take it." Now, he is still the manager; there is no director. Everyone knows he is honest and capable. He sells books at moderate prices. Sometimes he uses money to print notebooks to distribute to pupils.

What we want to do is to bring out beautiful books, interesting books; and that's all. Now he says, not only to me but to all our friends, "I want to go back to the countryside to farm now, because people don't have money to buy books anymore." So all of us say, "Please hang on. Although you cannot sell as many as before, a work like this cannot just stop."

BERRIGAN: It seems to me that when these monks take a position in regard to the Thieu government or refuse to serve in the military, when they go to prison and suffer as we know so many of them do, and when they begin hunger fasts and so on, everything in their lives prepares them for such a position. They have very little to lose; they're independent, unattached to money and property. And so, they're ready to stand up for their beliefs when the machinery becomes oppressive.

NHAT HANH: Yes, it is not a great sacrifice. For people like that to be jailed is much easier than to wear the uniform and carry a gun. They have been taught that they shouldn't kill even a mosquito, and they can't. They have nothing to lose. They cannot be incited by fear of Communism.

BERRIGAN: In fact, there's a deep connection between the way these men are living and what Communism says the ideal way of life is. If Communism is true to itself, it says, "Share your property and be poor and work for others, and make your life one of service." It seems to me that these monks are already living the life of an ideal society. They're already living in opposition to all kinds of oppression, wealth, money. So when the monks are true to their own tradition, they're bringing about an ideal society. In opposing societies that exist for the rich, for the military, and for killing, it's hard for me to see that there should be any trouble with Communism.

NHAT HANH: To put the ideal to work is the thing that can prove hardest. Something prepared us. Because in the monastic life you are free to be poor, to share, and you can find your own way. These monks—they cannot be manipulated by fear or hatred.

BERRIGAN: That's a great victory. It seems to me that you're describing a religious tradition which is still as vital as it ever was—maybe even better than it was in certain periods.

I think we're learning that the West is in the last days of a system which has already proven itself antihuman and bankrupt, and this includes the last days of the church as we know it. The church has entirely meshed its destiny and method with that of capitalism and the military. Once you get beyond the religious talk, its institutions are no different. All are making money off the misery of people elsewhere in the world, and are helping weapons systems be created.

Whereas, as I understand it, the Buddhists have grasped the future. By being faithful to simple things now, Buddhism hasn't become part of something that must die, or that must be ended, the way the church in the West has. This is part of the torment of younger people, I think, who have some religious hope, who would like to identify with the Catholic church or with Judaism. But they find that they're being mobilized into a system which is part of the death system. Being a religious person will not free them to form the future. It's only by cutting loose from both church and state that they can become free people. Whereas, I think in Vietnam one can be authentic and a Buddhist and part of a continuity.

NHAT HANH: Although, the Buddhist community has certainly not been without corruption. The corruption always comes in periods of trouble or during periods of glory. For instance, when Buddhism has a lot of prestige, many people join the pagodas because they want to identify themselves with that glory. When the pagodas are too big and too crowded, then there arise elements that do not live according to the Buddhist ideal. Always like that. And in periods when there is hunger, many people become Buddhist monks too, because in the Buddhist temples they get tax exemptions for the land; and in the temple they will have a chance to survive, although everybody knows that the life of a monk in a monastery is most austere. Parents don't want their sons to become monks; it's a hard life. You live in a community, and you just get one or two vegetarian meals a day.

There are a number who join the pagodas because they don't want to be drawn into a war. We cannot say this is because of their cowardice; I think nobody wants to kill anyway, especially when a war is not fought to preserve independence. So, among the six hundred monks who are in prison, there may be some who became monks just to resist being drafted. But even now they prefer jail to the army. I think the monasteries must be open to receiving such people, to protect others from being drawn into the war.

BERRIGAN: But it seems to me that the very difficult times mainly purify the religious tradition; the good times corrupt it. When the church is enjoying a kind of normal condition, a normal relationship with the state, it often tends to have no vitality. Yet when some Christians are in prison or in trouble, there can be a very important renewal, much more than Vatican Councils, World Conferences, can bring about.

I also wanted to compare the relationship of the Vietnam government to the monks with the relationship of the government in the United States to monks. I couldn't imagine, in the worst days of the war, that the government would invade the monastery of Merton and drag out the monks and throw them into prison. They would much rather leave them there because they know that those monks are saying their prayers and working hard, that they just don't signify, that they have no political meaning to the government. But there must have been something very different going on in Buddhist pagodas for the government to take these terrible steps.

NHAT HANH: Oh, because Buddhist temples have become strongholds of resistance.

Sometimes the monks have had to barricade themselves in with chairs and tables, and as a weapon they threw pepper at the invaders. The Diem government raided several pagodas and took all the monks to prisons. They carried the monks far away, close to the border of Cambodia. On the twentieth of August, 1963, toward midnight, all the temples that were strongholds of the resistance for the country were raided.

BERRIGAN: But you see, I'm still puzzled as to the conception of a monk's life that leads a monastery to become a center of resistance in one culture. In our culture, the monastery is just a monastery—no interest in the government, no interest in the war. Do you see what I mean?

NHAT HANH: Maybe we are more on the spot. It hurts us too much. We have to react.

BERRIGAN: To the war?

NHAT HANH: Yes. To war and to oppression. You know, we had thought that the monks in Cambodia would never demonstrate like we did in Vietnam, because they listen too much to the government. But recently, the monks in Cambodia have gone by the thousands to demonstrate, for the situation has become different, and it hurts the religious communities.

BERRIGAN: How?

NHAT HANH: Bombing. All kinds of things. But I think in the United States there are places where you can just be quiet.

BERRIGAN: The war is not in our country; it's "somewhere else."

NHAT HANH: It's too far away. It's like strange stories, very far away. A kind of isolation. We knew that when we transformed our temple into a resistance stronghold, we could no longer merely meditate. What do you meditate upon if not the sufferings of yourself, of your own church? The problem is how to go on with the struggle and yet still have time to be yourself, to continue your spiritual life. But, the spiritual life does not need to be led in a quiet totally detached way.

BERRIGAN: I used to have the idea, when I was young and naïf, that people who dedicated their lives to God would be very peaceable and would oppose war. I can remember the first time I received a severe shock. I had gone to a convent of contemplative nuns in New Jersey to give a talk. I said that during time of war monks and nuns had a very special call. Their call was to be aware and, if possible, to go where people were suffering and dying—to go to the center of war, and to find out how to be a nun or a monk there, and not to stay apart. Well, the reaction to this little talk, which I thought simple and logical, was a terrific, negative reaction.

I began to realize that you could not take life in the abstract and say that contemplative people are going to be superior in their moral insights and are going to sense the transcendent character of life more clearly nor are they going to be more protective of innocent people. I saw that these people were joined to a complex network of social and political attitudes. Even though they did a lot of praying, they still were quite hawkish. They were patriotic, in a terrible sense; they were no different from anybody else. Some were thoughtful and moral, acute about questions of life. And others were living in some war situation out of their own past or some conception of patriotism that was quite un-Christian. Then I began to notice, every time I went to a monastery after that, there were these same divisions among the monks—the same divisions we had outside. It wasn't the case that the most spiritually-aware peo-

ple were in monasteries. There was the same mix as in society
outside. For me it was a very sharp, unexpected discovery, and
it took a good deal of time to absorb it.

NHAT HANH: I always think of monasteries as places where
one works out spiritual matters, like laboratories where scien-
tists work on new discoveries. If people feel the need to be in
a monastery for one year, or two or three years, we must have
places for them to go, just to live, to look into themselves in
order to see things more clearly.

BERRIGAN: I think that comparison very true. But you understand what I've been trying to say about the substratum of
attitudes that can go unchallenged in a monastery. People
think that they're doing something radical by going into a
monastery because they've turned their back on society. But
monasteries also have their taboos, their false traditions, and
their stereotyped attitudes. One cannot automatically say,
"I got reborn because I went into a monastery." One has to
also become free in the monastery. In becoming a monk, one
is not always returning to a primitive, fresh understanding of
religion. One may well be entering a parallel institution, parallel to the society.

It takes a long time and a lot of courage to find that out, and
then to react so that the realization becomes a step in one's
rebirth. It took me many years, for instance, to realize the un-
conscious, unexplained links with the culture which were still
binding me, in the Jesuit order. Everyone said that when you
go into the order you become free, free to follow the Gospel;
but this is not true. You enter another institution that can also
be enslaving.

So a monk, East or West, still has to find out for himself,
with the help of others, what are the real roots of life and
whether or not he is going to be a true son of his tradition, a
true brother. That doesn't always follow just because one
wears this or that clothing or follows a particular regime. It's
very difficult today to be a human being—anywhere today.
And "human being" ought, one thinks, to define a monk.

I think it was the war that shook me into these realizations.
I wouldn't say that it shook many of us. Great numbers of

our priests and monks still believe that to be a good American is a very important thing; and they believe it in a bad way, a very negative way. They still see their lives in terms of professional competence and professional status, and not much more than that. But, for some of us the war really came home. We had to take a new look at our lives, and that was good, even though it was very difficult.

It's a great aid, as you describe it, to be in a society where the majority of your people are poor and where there aren't these incredible forces at work which inevitable drive the church to enrich itself, to gain more material possessions.

NHAT HANH: The real Buddist cannot be rich.

BERRIGAN: Why is that?

NHAT HANH: If you have compassion, you cannot be rich.

BERRIGAN: You could say that about the real Christian. But they all get rich. Not all, many.

NHAT HANH: Maybe it's not that all poor Christians are more Christian or poor Buddhists are real Buddhists. But it seems that compassion, both in Buddhism and in Christianity, is so important, so basic, that you can be rich only when you can bear the sight of suffering. If you cannot bear that, you have to give your possessions away.

BERRIGAN: Still, there must be Buddhists who make compromises just as there are Christians who make compromises.

NHAT HANH: Sure, sure. Maybe the difference is that our country is not very wealthy. When somebody is rich, he is not very rich when compared to a rich Christian. But it's like corruption, it's not because you can steal more that you are more corrupted.

BERRIGAN: But because you can steal.

NHAT HANH: So you cannot say that in our country corruption has not happened.

Poverty applies not only to monks and nuns, but also to laymen. There is the doctrine of self-sufficiency, the limit of your needs, and if you have more than what you really need, you are not exercising temperance. The purpose of this virtue is to have more time to work for your spiritual growth and for the sake of others. If you only think and work to accumulate riches for yourself, and do not know when to stop, that is not temperance. As far as Buddhist community goes, it's a Communist way of life. The bases are the six principles of communal life: to observe the same discipline, to share the same roof, to share one's understanding and knowledge, to reconcile different viewpoints, and to avoid disputes by kind words. The last is the vow to hold all property in common. You take only what you need; the rest is for the community. It began more than twenty-five hundred years ago. It was the basis of monastic life during the time of Buddha and it has been observed very closely since.

BERRIGAN: Through this monastic example, laypeople also have been influenced in their use of material things?

NHAT HANH: The doctrine should be applied by laypeople as far as economic need allows.

8

Jesus
and
Buddha

NHAT HANH: I always think that to be able to look into the eyes of one true Master is worth one hundred years studying His doctrine, His teaching. In Him you have a direct example of enlightenment, of life, while in others you have only a shadow, which may help you also, but not directly. As the Buddha says, "My doctrine is only a raft helping to bring you over to the other shore, not ultimate reality; you shouldn't worship it."

BERRIGAN: Well, how do you look into the eyes of Jesus or the Buddha?

NHAT HANH: How? Well, there's no how. It's like asking, How do I look at you? How do I look at a branch of a tree? The problem is not how, but the subject who does the looking. Because if you put in front of people one thing, and you have many people come and look at it, they see different things. It depends not only on the thing you exhibit but on the nature and the substance of the one who looks. So when you are in direct touch with reality, you have more chance to break into it rather than when you have just an image of reality; that's the map and not the city, the shadow not the tree, the doctrine and not the savior, life. There are those who look into the eyes of the Buddha, into the eyes of Jesus, but who are not capable of seeing the Buddha or Jesus. I think that is quite hopeless.

We have a number of stories in Buddhist literature of the many people who came from very far in hope that they might be able to see the Buddha. But they could not see the Buddha because of the way they reacted to things they had seen on the way. One such man met a woman who needed help, but he was in such a hurry to see the Buddha that he neglected the child of the helpless widow. Of course he could not see the Buddha. So I say that whether you can see the Buddha or not depends very much on you.

BERRIGAN: It is amazing how many of these insights there are across different lives and cultures and traditions. One thinks of that shattering scene of judgment at the end of Matthew's Gospel when the Lord says, "So long" to some people because they didn't feed Him and clothe Him and visit Him in prison. They all say, "How come?" And he says, "You didn't do it to my brothers. Too bad. So long."

It's a deep question to me: how do you meet the eyes of Jesus or the Buddha? Probably the question of a dumb novice; still, I think that if people could breathe with the silence of Jesus something would happen. He spent a lot of His life silently. If only one could go into the desert with Jesus or be in prison with Him during Holy Week or penetrate to His silence before Pilate and Herod, when He refused to answer, as another way of answering. It seems to me these are profound meetings, moments which go beyond the necessity of a lot of palaver. I often think of the meaning of a monk, like yourself or Merton or the young monk whose death we heard about today. These are people who have met the eyes of Jesus or Buddha through some understanding of silence.

NHAT HANH: When I spoke of looking into the eyes of Buddha, I was thinking of the Buddha as a human being who is surrounded by special atmosphere. I notice that great humans bring with them something like a hallowed atmosphere, and when we seek them out, then we feel peace, we feel love, we feel courage.

Maybe only an image can explain this. The Chinese say, "When a sage is born, the water in the river and the plants and trees on the mountains nearby become clearer and more green." It is their way of talking about the milieu that is born at the same time as a holy being.

In Buddhism we talk of *karma* as a fruit or as a seed. The karma seed is action-being and the karma fruit is what you get, the concoction of all your deeds and your thoughts and your being. So, *karmaphala* is the fruit of karma. It consists of two parts: the first is yourself, and the second part is the milieu that surrounds you. When you come and stay one hour with us, you bring that milieu—a kind of *rayonnement* which comes from yourself. It is as though you bring a candle into this room. The candle is there; there is a kind of light-zone you bring in.

When a sage is there and you sit near him, you feel light, you feel peace. That is why I said that if you sit close to Jesus and look into His eyes and still don't see Him, that's hopeless, because in such a case you have much more chance to see, to be saved, to get enlightenment, than when you read His teachings. Of course, if He's not there, His teaching is next best.

When I read and hold the scriptures, whether Buddhist or Christian, I always try to be aware of the fact that when the Buddha or Jesus said something, they were saying it to someone or to some group of people. I should understand the circumstances in which they spoke, in order to get into communion with them rather than merely take their saying word for word. If I have a story to tell an adult, I can tell it to a child too. But I would tell the story differently to a child— not because I want to do so, but because I'm facing a child. So my story naturally takes another form. I believe that what the Buddha said, what Jesus said, is not as important as the *way* the Buddha or Jesus said it. If you are able to perceive that, you will get close to the Buddha or to Jesus. But if you try to analyze, try to find out the deep meaning of the words without realizing the kind of relationship between the one who spoke and those who listened, I think that you very easily miss not only the point but the man. I think that theologians tend to forget that approach.

BERRIGAN: This strikes me, coming out of seminary teaching. I used to meet these theologians, I didn't know what to say to them because I didn't understand them. One learned man I used to meet in the elevator. I knew he was giving lectures around the country; the subject was "The Idea of Love in the New Testament." I thought that was a strange thing to talk about—the *idea* of love. I thought he might talk about love in the New Testament, you know, instead of the *idea* of God, the *idea* of this, the *idea* of that. I thought one reason for the deep trouble among the students at the seminary was that there was no atmosphere around them inviting them to become Christians. Rather, the atmosphere was urging them to become experts in Christianity. And the two are very different things. This was simply not working. It was not working for their lives, so many were leaving. They were refusing to be ordained. Many were staying on, but were unhappy and dissatisfied.

But it seemed to me that any professor of Christianity who could keep his life uninterrupted and untroubled during the last decade of the Vietnam war could only bring trouble to students. At the very least he would be offering the bad example of one who was only talking about "The Idea of the New Testament" instead of conveying the atmosphere of Jesus. A terrifying abstraction. I'm not thinking of an intellectual failure; that's an abstraction too. What I'm really considering is that the reality of Jesus has been submerged to the point where all kinds of aberrations are in the air about Him. And the first aberration is the one taught by the theologians: "The Idea of Jesus."

Then there are these other aberrations, more popular ones, involving Jesus freaks. This is a sign, it seems to me, of the break between generations; a true tradition has been lost. Younger people, through some splintered notions, are still desperately grabbing some aspect of Jesus. Because part of the whole Western tradition is Jesus, He cannot be entirely lost. But what they can grab is so partial and distorted that they look at Jesus and forget the world. You know? But in that, they're not very much different from the professors at the seminary who also, purportedly at least, look at the idea of Jesus and forget the world [Laughter]. At least the kids are beyond the idea. But both sides are doing violence to Jesus.

NHAT HANH: Speaking of violence, the Buddha was born in a society that was less overtly violent than the society in which Jesus was born. But you read the scripture and you see that the Buddha was very, very strong. His reaction to the Veda traditions was total; He denied the whole thing. The idea of Atma or self is the center, the kernel, of the Veda and of the Upanishads. But the teaching of the Buddha was based on the idea of non-Atma. That means a reaction. Not because "non-self" is so important that the Buddha used it as the foundation of His teaching. But the teaching began as a reaction against the stagnation of life in His society. And yet, He was not crucified; the Indians didn't do such things. But, I'm sure that if the Buddha were born in the society where Jesus was born, He would have been crucified also.

Again, you may think that Buddha was more direct in His reactions than Christ, but this is not true. This is just because in His milieu, another way was possible. With Jesus, we see His tremendous courage, facing that society and trying to break out of that kind of life, that kind of existence, which is not life at all. If there is a lack of understanding of circumstances, you just do not see the facts straight.

The Buddha began with the idea of nonself, really a reaction against His time. But many Buddhists think that nonself, non-Atma, is the basis of all truth. In this, they are considering a means to be an end, a raft to be the shore, the finger pointing to be the moon. There has to be something more important than nonself—which is the nonattachment to both nonself and self. The self that people of Buddha's time used to worship was the real cause of social injustice, through ignorance, through stagnation. Society was full of evils; the system of castes, the control of life by the Brahmans, the treatment of the untouchables, the monopolization of spiritual teaching by people who enjoyed the best material conditions and who were not spiritual at all. Such people were farthest from reality, but they still claimed to be the representatives of the Absolute.

So, Buddhism was a way of reacting. It was not an attempt to present reality in terms of a doctrine, in the form of a doctrine. That is why for Buddhists to be attached to a doctrine, even a Buddhist doctrine, is to betray the Buddha. Such people are not capable of seeing the Buddha. In the *Diamond Sutra*, Buddha was quoted as having said, "If you try to see me through form and in sounds, then you shall not see me." I think the "sounds" are also the doctrine, attachment to the doctrine and to the views.

I remember a student asking me about the lotus position— if that was the perfect position. I answered him that there was no question of a perfect position. I said it was unnecessary to create an ideal position. But I hoped that if he wanted he could create one without imitating the Chinese and Japanese in their way.

Buddha said, "Well, you think that there is an identity, an absolute identity, in things. I say that things are empty, that kind of identity does not exist. If you look for an absolute identity of a chair, I say that it is empty." Then people began to worship the idea of emptiness; He said, "It is worse if you believe in the nonself of a chair than if you believe in the self of a chair." Do you see? It is not the words and the concepts that are important but something within; the way to deal with things, to be with humans, is important.

BERRIGAN: "Something within" seems to have stood the Buddhists in very good stead.

NHAT HANH: The world of today is no longer the world of yesterday, when each country, each group of people, could live separately. Our karma now has come together, has become collective karma. Now the action of one group affects the other group. We must choose to suffer together or be happy together, be alive together or be destroyed together.

BERRIGAN: The closing of a circle; this is also the revenge of the karma. To live this way, in this international prison, and to be satisfied with this type of life is a terrible punishment against reality, inflicted on those who have spurned reality.

It's hard to know where the breaking of this iron ring can be done, where its weak point is. My feeling is that the ring will tighten until it just breaks apart at every point because it's equally strangling at every point, like a circle tightening around your throat. But, of course, meantime the tragedy is that Americans are being strangled slowly, but people elsewhere are being strangled quickly.

NHAT HANH: On the other hand, we notice another extreme. This touches on our efforts to support the victims of the war —children, widows, mutilated people, prisoners. Some look upon these as unimportant efforts; our work has been described by a number of people as not intelligent enough, not in the direction of liberation or revolution. Many of our troubles in doing our work have come from such attitudes. Often religious and political groups only aim at preserving the identity of their own group, facing a threat from another group. Each side has that kind of fear. Why don't we join together and deal with the real threat?

In fact, an identity can be an identity only when there are things that describe it as a nonidentity. To return to the example of the identity of the chair, a chair can only exist in a non-chair context. If we look carefully at a chair we can see the trees from where the wood came, the human race from where the carpenter came and so on. The relationship between self and nonself is such that the self exists only when the nonself exists. In a Buddhist sutra, the Buddha described this in a very simple way. He said, "This is, because that is. This is not, because that is not." So, all things rely on each other in order to be. My identity meets your identity in order to be possible. Why don't we come together in order to find ways to preserve not only my identity but your identity and that of others too?

Resistance against boundaries, against the setting up of false frontiers and limitations, is so important. Not only should people in the community *profess* to overcome these, but they should overcome them by their *way* of being there. Unfortunately, once we identify ourselves with something such as a nation, an ideology, or a religious faith, we tend to think of all the other things as not important or not true.

For example, we've gotten many tragic reports that are generally ignored in the West. A mother despaired when she heard her children ask every morning why the soup was so thin. She couldn't bear it. So, one evening she put all the rice that was left into the pan and made a thick soup. But she also put poison in it. Mother and children ate and died. And yet, in such a situation we are still forced to take up guns, to kill each other. The suffering of Vietnam, has it offered a lesson to America? Has it helped Americans to reexamine their self-image? Does it help at all?

BERRIGAN: I have some hope. I don't think we really know yet. I sense that there are deep changes occurring, just breaking through here and there, still having no public expression either in political life or in public structures. So, we're in that twilight world.

9

Communities
of
Resistance

NHAT HANH: Tell me, how do you see the possibility of developing and maintaining communities of resistance in the United States and elsewhere? We have not talked about that.

BERRIGAN: But, it seems to me, everything we've talked about leads naturally to that.

I think there's not much else other than these communities on the horizon, and not much else worth giving one's energy to. I'm very fortunate in having in my own family and friends examples of such community, and I'm sure you do too. I guess the question is one of encouraging and enlarging all of this; you know, realizing that the sixties are by no means a finished decade but that they set in motion a pattern of violence, as well as a counterforce of nonviolence which must be maintained. I have the deepest conviction that a sane and reasonable religious sense has the resources to bring these communities into being and to maintain them. There are other bases from which to start—but I know this way. I know this is a good way. I know what it can do.

The more I move around, the more I realize that whatever I do should be judged in its relationship to these communities. I think I'm drawn more and more into the understanding that the future, if we want to talk about the future in a real and concrete way, will include this form of community.

NHAT HANH: I hope to see communities like that everywhere, as a kind of demonstration that life is possible, a future is possible. Someone has said that cities are places where humans are the only living beings; there are no trees, no animals, no other kinds of living beings, no nature. There is a lack of balance. And then there are many things that regulate us, rob us of our serenity, our peace, our time, ourselves. So, a community that shows abundance of life, that is an example of the wholeness of life, would be an eloquent sign of the possibility of the future. I believe that in such a community, one person could signify hope and life sufficiently to maintain the community.

I don't know what kind of rapport such a community could have with existing monastic communities—whether it could learn from them, whether there could be a mutual sharing. In certain monastic communities such changes are under way, in order to arrive at wholeness. What can the church do in order to encourage and support a community life which is simple and alive?

BERRIGAN: These are very deep waters. I have had these ideas for a long time and never got anywhere with them except with Merton. And it's interesting that so much of his dream waited on his death. It's only after his death that these communities of resistance are springing up in his name, inspired by his writing and his life. But, I would think that the more we can break down the wall between—*monastic* maybe is an unfortunate word because it's not common coin. Community, in our case Christian community, includes degrees of, rhythms of, withdrawal and involvement, withdrawal and urban dedication and international dedication—all of these things. And the worst thing that can happen to monks is that they get convinced that they're different from ordinary poeple. That's very bad on both sides. The worst thing that can happen to Christian or Buddhist laypeople, I would think, is that they begin to say, "Well, the monks are so different that there's nothing to talk about, nothing to share."

Still the walls are there and the walls are high, at least in the West. I must say I have never been attracted to the monastery since Merton died. I never felt that there was a spirit that would be sympathetic to what I was trying for. You know, this is a great tragedy. My friends who have visited the monastery since he died say it's not a very interesting place. And we've appreciated more and more the deep pain of Merton's struggle to try to stay with that community and still to speak to the world. Well, maybe this is not terribly to the point, but the number of monks who are deeply conscious of the pain of the world is small—at least in the sense that they know they have something to offer to heal that pain. This is, I feel, a great loss to them and to us. I have so often said to young monks, "Try to think that you are not planted somewhere like a tree, but are on pilgrimage, back and forth; one who goes and comes back and offers to our people the resources of discipline and wisdom which are your gifts; gifts which, I think, are bottled into a monastery vintage and are simply not available to us." But it is difficult for this to be heard, very difficult.

NHAT HANH: In our tradition, monasteries are only a kind of laboratory to spend time in, in order to discover something. They're not an end, they're a means. You get training and practice of the spiritual life so that you can go elsewhere and be with other people. In our special situation where the war has been a terrible reality, the monks have really been with the people. Both monks and laypeople have made efforts to find a form of community that is more fitted to our need. A number of friends and I have tried a new community. It was successful because, I think, it grew out of the tradition, because most who came to the community had undergone some training in monasteries. But our community, well, we made it very different. There was absolutely no rule, no discipline.

And we also accepted non-monks—writers and artists—to be residents for months or years. That worked well, I think, because the people who came there had the same kind of need. We didn't need an abbot or a monastic rule.

Unfortunately, the war finally prevented us from continuing. But that too proved a blessing. Many of the young monks and nuns have cooperated with the peasants to form new communities where they work the land like the other people.

They also have days and hours of meditation, studies, and recitation of sutras and prayer. Without that it would be hard for them to continue. We also tried a new order, an order that would be easier for the young people to join and to feel at home in. You know, Nhat Chi Mai, the girl who burned herself—she belonged to that order. In that order, you are supposed to have ninety days a year—three months—of contemplative life. But you can space it the way you want it. And each week one day is left free.

BERRIGAN: That's nice. For flying kites? [Laughter]

NHAT HANH: Sure! And for reciting the book of discipline, meditation, and doing things you want like arranging flowers, reading poetry, and things like that.

BERRIGAN: Would you say a little something more about the rule that you decided on?

NHAT HANH: You know, in our tradition the monk's rules are 250 and the rule for the nuns, 100 more. That's called nuns' liberation! [Laughter] But for the new order there are only fourteen rules.

BERRIGAN: Ah! That's not too many.

NHAT HANH: And the idea is different, because they are more like guiding principles than rules. Each principle should be studied and applied with all one's strength. The first rule is about the worship of ideologies. "One should not be idolatrous or bound to any doctrine, any theory, any ideology, including Buddhist ones. Buddhist systems of thought must be guiding means and not absolute truth." There are principles to help us free ourselves from prejudices and listen to others and see reality and truth of different forms. The rule not to kill, however, does not come first.

BERRIGAN: That's interesting.

NHAT HANH: The rule says not to kill—not to kill and not to allow or encourage others to kill. And to do all you can in order to prevent killing and to prevent war. Concerning the problem of suffering, it is said in another principle—do not cut yourself off from suffering people, because that contact nourishes one's compassion. We also had a code of disciplines.

All this was to be reviewed every three years so it would fit the current situation. It is the spiritual life of the community that leads to change. The principle is only a manifestation of the spiritual life, and not something that conditions the spiritual life.

I think if we have peace in Vietnam, it still will be possible for us to build communities where we can live a simple and happy life. Because the country has not been industrialized, we still have time to avoid ruin in the direction of total industrialization.

For now, of course, the situation makes it impossible to think realistically of communities, unless one thinks also of resistance. Could you say something about the meaning of that expression— "communities of resistance"?

BERRIGAN: I think the word *resistance* became very important around 1967 in the States. People were saying that it was necessary to take a step beyond protest. We could no longer look upon our style of life as merely being an occasion for this or that action. People had to begin thinking much more seriously and deeply about a long term struggle in which they would stand up more visibly and perhaps with more risk. Of course, people saw that transition in quite a different way. Some of the political activists said that a moral, individual action was no longer enough; there must be unity of effort which was more and more highly political. One person refusing induction or going on trial or leaving the university would have no impact. Now there must be a community behind him.

Resistance, of course, was as ambiguous as the people who engaged in it. Some saw it as a violent word, some as nonviolent. I never heard the phrase "communities of resistance," as such, until around 1970; the word *resistance* around 1967 or 1968. But the idea developed that there would be communities, each member of which was dedicated to some violent or nonviolent ideal, some political or spiritual ideal, or some combination of these—political and spiritual.

I think it just to say that the roots of all this were among the religious people. I think they saw it first. Actually around that time, mainly as a result of Catonsville and the draft board actions, people began to say that it was not enough to perform one action and disperse. People had to stay together preparing for trial, talking around the country, preparing legal defense, raising money, educating other people. So the term arose out of those days after Catonsville. Communities of resistance were now required. I don't think a better term has been thought of.

NHAT HANH: I think that's a very meaningful term. And *resistance*, at root, I think, must mean more than resistance against war. It is a resistance against all kinds of things that are like war. Because living in modern society, one feels that he cannot easily retain integrity, wholeness. One is robbed permanently of humanness, the capacity of being oneself. When I drive through Paris, the noises and the traffic jams make me nervous. Once I have gone through Paris I become less than myself. And there are so many things like that in modern life that make you lose yourself. So perhaps, first of all, resistance means opposition to being invaded, occupied, assaulted, and destroyed by the system. The purpose of resistance, here, is to seek the healing of yourself in order to be able to see clearly. This may sound as though it falls short of a positive act of resistance. Nevertheless, it's very basic.

I think that communities of resistance should be places where people can return to themselves more easily, where the conditions are such that they can heal themselves and recover their wholeness.

BERRIGAN: Something to do with occupation and invasion. The New Testament refers to "possession," the possession of people by demons. A very powerful action of Jesus is the casting out of demons. And one of the meanings of Christian sanctuary is a place where the demons are not welcome. Once you pass into these precincts, you're free from the influence of the demonic and the possession by machinery and pseudo-values and hatred.

But I was thinking, too, that when Jesus cast out the demons, He often entered into conversation with the people about what this might mean—whether they were conscious of being possessed. He was, I think, trying to determine the exact power of the demon over this person, the degree of self-possession which the person still retained. And it was only afterward in many cases, I think, that this tactic of His was understood by those who either read the account or were present during the event.

Psychiatric theories tend to throw out exorcism as being a primitive form of magic, something we have outgrown. In fact, there is a profound lesson here about the possession, the invasion, the loss of soul, loss of self-understanding on the part of many modern people. In the form almost of madness, one is invaded by the demonic values of this world, and runs with them.

Then the Book of Revelation extends all of that and says you don't really understand as long as you think it is only the person who is invaded. We must also see that there is an invasion of institutions and that the believing community is a charmed circle that withstands invasion. It is not an institution. First of all, it is a community; and secondly, this community lives by values which are utterly foreign to the values some men and women are possessed by. Thus, this community lives without attachment to money and prestige and hatred and violence and war. Its house will be buffeted and struck by the blows of the world; it can't exist in Nirvana in the sense of cheap grace. It has to earn its salvation by its love of the dispossessing Lord.

NHAT HANH: The church was first founded, I think, as a community of resistance.

BERRIGAN: I think so.

NHAT HANH: Yes. But finally, it couldn't resist and was invaded and possessed, and that is why new communities of resistance have to begin again.

A pagoda, a temple, a church, is built in a way that when you enter you recover yourself; you come into contact with the absolute reality, with God, with Buddha, with Buddhahood. And that is why the recovering of self is seen in architecture, in decorative art, in sacred music, in many things like that. So that when you come to the church or the temple you are helped by these things to return to yourself. I think that our communities of resistance should be built like a church or a temple where everything you see expresses the tendency to be oneself, to go back to oneself, to come into communion with reality. I believe that if that basic step is realized, then the second and third steps of resistance can be realized.

I look for communities of resistance—beautiful, healing, refreshing both in surroundings and in substance. In such communities you meet people who symbolize a kind of freshness; their look, their smile, their understanding, should be able to help. That is why a requirement of a community of resistance is the presence of at least one person who can offer that kind of atmosphere. Because of him or her you want to go back. I suggest that a community like that should, if possible, arise in a place that has pleasant surroundings. And there should be someone there in residence, so that when people think of him or her they feel some encouragement, some hope. The place should be identified with such a person. So even if that person is not there, when people come near the place, they would like to drop in. Because they know that person has been sitting under that tree. When I come and sit under that tree I feel the presence of a friend.

I'm not saying that a movement should be built on one person. But I think that if you want two persons, you should have one person first. A small brother always has need of a big brother during a certain period of time. I say this out of my own experience.

BERRIGAN: There are things, I think, peculiar to America which are very difficult to cope with, and which I don't think are experienced here in Paris, much less in Vietnam. There is the hyperconsciousness of young Americans about elitism which makes for a very uneasy relationship with someone who's older, expecially someone who is famous or a media person—even though this person may resist all that. I think young people uneasily oscillate between admiration for a person like that and great distrust of him. This makes the situation on both sides very uneasy. It is difficult to be yourself because the media are invading, claiming one. It becomes a great source of difficulty to identify in a genuine fashion with a community of young people if you're trying to remain true to the struggle. At the same time, one is not at their stage of things because one is older and better known and is trying to be faithful to many different tasks. It would be easier if one chose, say, either of two things: I'm just going to travel and talk and write; or I'm just going to forget all that and stay with one community. But neither of these, I think, is a good solution. Somehow you find some uneasy way of being faithful to both aspects: people who ask you to go elsewhere, and the community that asks you to work at home. It's complex.

NHAT HANH: I think all of us should overcome that kind of prejudice about people: leadership, fame, authority, prestige. Because none of that is important. Once I met a young student who sat with me for a while but didn't say anything. I began a conversation; he said, "It's so difficult to talk to you because you are well-known." I said, "I think that's silly, and it's your fault. It's not my fault because it's not my intention to sit far away from you." If you sit near a person and you find some pleasant feeling, that's good; you don't need anything more. The pleasant feeling and the communication that you establish—that's all you need.

BERRIGAN: What became of your community in Vietnam? Where are those members now?

NHAT HANH: All scattered. Everyone still remembers the community, though the community is no longer there because of the war. But the task was, and is, a big one; many of us, thanks to it, have had occasion to be healed. Our wounds were very, very deep before we created the community. We established ourselves far away from the village, on a mountain in the deep forest. And we spent years there in order to heal ourselves. Because we were together, we created a kind of relationship that still exists to this day, even though we are scattered all over Vietnam and, in the case of Phuong and myself, exiled overseas. Everyone is still trying to do his best, but more or less in the same direction; and we feel the presence of each other.

That was only the first step of a community of resistance; the community of resistance should go beyond. The things

Philip and Elizabeth and their friends are doing show other aspects of such communities. What I am thinking just now is that the two aspects we just discussed should complete each other, should help each other. It's our task to try to set up communities which are expressing life, reality, and are doing active resistance work.

BERRIGAN: I think so, yes. Too bad the monasteries, at least in Europe and the United States, don't see their task in this way. The trouble is that monasteries have become pleasant places where discipline and prayer go on, but where resistance does not go on. So today there is practically no conception of a monk or a nun who is a resisting person. In the States one has to say, though, that the nuns have moved remarkably in this direction, but usually against the understanding of their orders. The men have not followed this to any degree. I must say even with Merton it was a struggle to convince him that it was possible to be a monk in a way which was also actively resisting. He was in and out of that idea for many, many years, right up to his death. But the monks who will carry that idea forward—I don't know if they even exist.

NHAT HANH: If in many monastic communities people are praying and meditating but do not resist, maybe it's because they do not pray and meditate properly. Because, I think, the object of praying and meditating is life—life in the most beautiful, glorious meaning of the word. The existence of Buddhism, of Christianity, and other religious disciplines has to do with life, with reality. When someone says that belief in Jesus is life, what life is he thinking of? The same kind of life that Jesus lived; it is the life which He suffered. So, meditating and praying should be in the context of life. And if you isolate yourself from the reality of suffering, I think that something is wrong.

Suppose there is a Buddhist temple in a village. The temple is not bombed, but the whole village has been bombed. People cry and weep and run about; the monks pray and meditate because the pagoda has not been bombed. I don't think such a situation can exist. I think the monks will both meditate and help a child who is wounded or meditate and help carry a wounded citizen out of the war zone, at the same time.

BERRIGAN: One would think in the right order of things that the monks would be the first to understand an historical situation which is morally intolerable—a war, above all else. That their discipline, their prayer, would render them acutely aware of what is occurring and intuitive about what to do. But this seems to be almost never verified. At least in my country the monks, except for very, very few, were among the last to come to any real understanding of things. They were the ones, in a sense, who resisted the resistance because they stood on their platonic trust in prayer as such, Mass as such, or divine office and chant as such, apart from any human intervention. They're always expecting God to intervene without their own intervention. The suppositions are very disturbing: real estate, land, buildings, remain untouched, undisturbed, uninvaded by suffering. The monks see themselves as men who pray in order that others do something. They pray in order that others "do God's will," as they say, that others suffer well, or others bear with prison. But the idea that their lives will be ground up is something very, very rare. And the realization that such a view of life is disincarnate, a betrayal of any real understanding of Christianity—that is very slow in coming.

NHAT HANH: I mentioned the case of a bombed village. Not only should the monks have been aware of the suffering after the village was bombed, but even before. The resistance should have started before the bombing. The community of resistance is not only to back up the people who resist, to back them up in some kind of political way. It is a kind of fortress. Excuse me for using this word! I'm thinking of a fortress for resistance; because of the threat of being invaded, one has to resist.

BERRIGAN: I like the idea of the two aspects of the community. When I was in Ireland I saw a few of the towers the monks raised at the time of invasions in the ninth and tenth centuries. Once I walked in the country and came on one of these great circular towers on a hill and saw, around it, the ruins of a monastery.

The monks built these towers during the Dark Ages so that something could be saved. When the northern barbarians came down, driving everyone before them, burning and raping and destroying, the monks went into the tower. I remember standing inside this tower, this incredible building that stood for nine centuries and withstood successive waves of destruction and barbarism. The monks felt they should save something. They saved the people from the countryside; they lived in those towers for months. And they took with them (the historians say) two things: the books and the sacred vessels. The books symbolized the tradition, the story of their past, where they came from, who they were; and the vessels were the mystery, the Eucharist. Another way of saying who they were, that trust could not be broken, keeping the command of Christ— do this, do this, keep this going, don't allow this to be destroyed. And then when the worst was over, they came out again.

Everything else was gone, except love! Obviously one doesn't continue to resist unless one has a vision; it's ridiculous to think so. If one has only politics to resist politics, then everything goes! If one has an ideology to resist an ideology, everything goes. What is required to resist the barbarian is a vision, a tradition, a faith; everything else goes except the people, the community, the symbols of salvation.

After a great deal of ignorance on my part, mistakes, getting nowhere with community, I like Bonhoeffer's statement that the community is a gift and that in certain circumstances community will not happen. It's not a question of blaming anybody; it is very mysterious. But I don't think you can make a community happen.

You know, when I came out of jail, I was invited to teach at a seminary in New York. This was an interesting place, with Protestants and Catholics together. Much work had gone into creating this ecumenical arrangement where the Jesuits and Protestants would teach together and learn together. After a while, the superiors in Rome became uneasy about certain aspects of the community; so they unexpectedly ordered the place closed. And this was our best seminary in the country. As a result, there was a great sense of betrayal, a sense of alienation and shock.

I thought that here was a stroke of lightning in the darkness, where suddenly you see the real structure of something. If a tree is hit by lightning, it flares up and you see things you hadn't seen before. What I saw was that this community was not a community at all; after the shock wore off, everyone began making other plans—where we should go to teach, where we should go to study. Suddenly it was all over—something that people had worked for years to create.

And I saw that we were just like Cornell University; we were an arrangement of convenience among professional people to do a certain job. Once that job was interrupted or made impossible or finished, people moved on. But there were no human roots there, and whatever pain arose was felt for reasons that were quite peripheral to the main issue, which I thought was, Do we really have a kind of organic happening here? Have people found something profound about worship, about common faith, about stewardship, sharing, service? Is this something so precious that people are not going to have it destroyed automatically by some command from above? When I saw there was no response of that kind at all, it was very painful. I felt that if this thing can be brought down so quickly and easily, it cannot be what I thought it was. And one must try again, try elsewhere. But that was a very painful awakening.

NHAT HANH: Sometimes a hasty judgment might lead you to cut off a relationship with a person. So, in my tradition we are taught to look at a tree or something like that for a long time. At first you don't know what use it is to look at a tree like that. You have to look until you can truly see it. And one day the tree reveals itself to you as a very substantial, real identity. It is not that you have a new tree or that the weather is better so that you can see the tree clearly, but something in oneself has changed so there is a new kind of relationship between you and the tree. Whether we can see the tree or not depends on us. Whether the tree can exist there or not depends on us. And whether one can be sad or sorrowful or joyful depends on the tree. So, a kind of wonderment arises. When I think of the relationship between two human beings, it's like that. It's not because you have some education that you can recognize a human being in his various aspects. You have to be with him and be with him a lot, and with a kind of open attitude, a kind of continuous self-transformation in you before such a relationship is possible, is fully realized.

I think that the encounter between man and God, the encounter between man and Buddhahood, reality, absolute reality, must be realized in the same way. It is not that the Buddha is more important than the tree. If you cannot have that kind of relationship with a tree, how can you expect to have it with the Buddha, with God, with ultimate reality?

I think that my contribution to the building of community life is to say, Do not judge each other too easily, too quickly, in terms of ideology, of point of view, strategies, things like that. Try to see the real person, the one with whom you live. You might discover aspects that will enrich you. It's like a tree that can shelter you.

But talking concretely, do you think that in countries like the United States it is still possible to create such communities? First, from the point of view of material needs, is it possible to set up the needed environment? And is it possible for a community living in that environment to produce what they need without having to rely too much on the outside? I ask you about the material aspect of building communities because we think it is still possible, in underdeveloped countries like ours, to build simple communities in which people live a simple life. Certainly this is possible in our south; because it's not cold, we can build very simple houses and wear simple clothes. And we can grow vegetables all year; there's no winter.

BERRIGAN: I don't think that the material question has ever been a very important one. In my experience, these communities can make it. If their sense of sacrifice and love of the community is alive, people always find ways of getting part-time work in a big city. You can work a few hours a day or some hours a week and be free; and then contribute that money to the others. There are friends who help, and there are cheap ways of living. Our failure has had nothing to do with material conditions. It's because we didn't have the guts or the heart to stay together to do serious work. One devastating difficulty is the mobility and pace which simply break people apart in the big cities, keep them from realizing and responding to the serious needs of others. I've never heard of any community that failed because it lacked material resources. Communities fail because they lack imagination and spiritual contact and soul and a sense of others and staying power and courage to move together and to live together.

NHAT HANH: I notice in a number of communities there are persons who are not very active. They don't lead at all. But because they are there, others like to go there. And these people are not talented or well-known; they are just very refreshing, very human. I think we need such people in each community.

BERRIGAN: Oh, absolutely. All this is part of the refreshing variety that is so required. We have in the States a few people who have actually become clowns. They have learned how to juggle, mime, do acrobatics and all kinds of things just in order to be with communities which are overwhelmed with serious work and ideology. They come and go with these communities. It's a very great help. I think that without a sense of humor, without laughter and jokes and a good time among themselves, people go insane. That was always the big thing in prison— being able to play the guitar, write poetry, recite poetry, and, in general, show that life was not sour.

But I was hoping we could say something also about the place of the family in these communities. If married people are part of this, marriage also would be an expression of resistance. In fact, the image of the family, it seems to me, should be the same as the image of the community of resistance. The community is a family of resistance which goes beyond blood into friendship.

NHAT HANH: And the existence of children is so refreshing and inspiring—the sight of a tiny baby, of very young children. One day I saw children playing; I felt so glad, so pleasant, I wrote Thomas Merton and said I hoped that he had time to watch children playing. He said, "Yes, you are right. Children are beautiful."

BERRIGAN: Is it true that in Vietnam the families have been

part of the nonviolent resistance?

NHAT HANH: Yes. Our community had all types of people—there were monks, writers, artists, and, from time to time, families came and stayed for weeks and months. In the Buddhist tradition there are two types of people who are responsible for the continuation of the church. One consists of those who live a contemplative life and stay in monasteries. After a period in monasteries, they find other places where they set up their own communities of learning and practice. They there are those who take care of the task of preaching and doing other kinds of work related to the church. There is a close relationship between these two. We have been trying to set up communities in which married and unmarried can be together, to abolish the separation between the two. Like the order we founded about ten years ago. Monastic people and married people observe the same discipline and share the same life in the community. And I notice that this arrangement is more relaxing; no discrimination, no complex of superiority or authority.

BERRIGAN: Did this order begin because of the war situation and its needs?

NHAT HANH: It was motivated by the need to actualize Buddhism, for Buddhism to be in the world, for the world; many such communities have arisen, to be of service in resistance. We notice in the order that living together and having time for meditation and sharing our feeling and experience—all this helped very much. If one was prevented from being with the community for a rather long time, he felt poorer for his absence; he could not perform his tasks as well as when he was together with his friends. It was so important; one's capacity to resist or to work was lessened very much by the lack of community life. Also one's faith was diminished.

BERRIGAN: Has any of these communities remained intact?

NHAT HANH: Well, everything has been hurt by the war. The most important and the biggest obstacle we encounter is the instability. In the village of Tra Lôc in Quang Tri, we went to live with the peasants. We settled there and helped them with our experiences in community building. We built quite a beautiful village. We called it a pilot village. Then it was destroyed. We built a second time, and it was destroyed a second time. Now they are trying to rebuild it again. Well, many people say, "Why do you build again and again? Go to other, more stable places." But the fact is that if we give up it is a very serious blow to us and our friends there, the peasants.

BERRIGAN: It sounds like the work of community itself: always being destroyed, always starting again. And the instability that you speak of doesn't strike us in the same way in the States; no villages or cities are bombed. It strikes people; people are bombed in their heads. People are so isolated and disrupted by the conditions of life that they cannot stay together. It's just as though their whole landscape were wiped out. Spiritually, if not physically, it becomes very difficult to continue. I think this is part of the trauma that we spoke of earlier, another form of the damage which continues to destroy people.

NHAT HANH: Do you think that it would be interesting to discuss the role of the community vis-à-vis personal religious experience? In other words, is it possible for an individual to find a way alone, to grow in his spiritual life?

BERRIGAN: It seems to me these are some of the most important questions facing us: just what resources are available, what discipline is required, and how people may come upon alternative ways of living today.

NHAT HANH: There is a feeling among people that they are incomplete if they are not with each other.

BERRIGAN: I think that feeling is everywhere. There is a terrifying and destructive loneliness, especially in the cities— people trying to make it alone, or merely touching the periphery of one another's lives. And there is a vacuum at the center of their existence. That certainly is experienced by those who have no community roots. But whether or not a destructive loneliness can lead to a better direction is a very difficult question. Loneliness itself, a kind of psychic amputation from others, does not imply that one is ready for the discipline of a community. In fact, it might imply just the opposite. I think it's very necessary to help and encourage a person to realize that certain things must be lost, certain ways given up, and certain attitudes confronted. This is a great purification which all are not capable of. In the kibbutz we visited near Tel Aviv, we asked, "Why do people leave the kibbutz, and why do people come?" The leader said, "Well, they come because they're lonely, and they leave because they're lonely." And we said, "Well what does that mean? How can they be lonely with three hundred people around them?" He explained, "They have never found a way of sharing their existence even while they're here." A certain common religious tradition is a very great help. That's why monks and nuns, it seems to me, should be natural initiators and helpers in forming communities; they themselves have undergone this discipline.

NHAT HANH: There is one resettlement village in Vietnam in which there are only three Catholic families, and the other 250 are Buddhist. But these Catholic families feel at home; they don't feel lonely. Maybe it is not necessary that all share the same religious ideals. What is important is that you find yourself in a situation where nobody discriminates. I think religions ought not separate people. (Yet there should be the particularity, the identity, of each group or each person.)

BERRIGAN: Of course we've seen instances where religion divides more than unites. This is an aspect of religion that should be reformed.

NHAT HANH: And even in a community where everyone professes the same social pattern, the same social aim, there is division.

BERRIGAN: Why? Is it because the disciplines they share are outmoded? Or because individual characters are so different they cannot fuse?

NHAT HANH: Of course there are many, many reasons, but there must be something that makes it more difficult now to live together than in the past. It may be that in the past, people had a feeling that they were already sure of their way. The way was there; for them it was only thinking of that way, advancing on that way. But in our time, the way has been very unclear, has required much searching.

BERRIGAN: When we became novices, for instance, there was

a supposition shared by all who came into the order. You came to receive a common vision, accepted by everyone. It was a matter of great pride and esteem to be a member of this order. And for many years you were to be trained, judged, evaluated. But there was a vision underlying it. I think everyone came in with a common expectation of the way life would go. You were going later to be part of this or that community doing this or that work—writing or teaching or abroad in mission work. It was all clearly defined, and the communities you went into also had their own character, which you were invited to share, to be initiated into. But it was only rarely that you were asked to initiate something new.

Then suddenly, about fifteen years ago, all of that changed. The common assumptions of the community collapsed, more or less. The younger people began to question deeply, began to leave, refused to be part of these old institutions. They demanded smaller communities and new work and much more of the responsibility for their own community. They asked to create as they went, rather than merely to inherit and take along this baggage. And that, of course, has been catastrophic for many people, especially for older people.

I think that in my order the present difficulty is twofold. Many give up and wander off into a culture which is not capable of satisfying their needs. Or, those who stay often settle for a kind of arrangement of convenience. They live together peaceably and do professional work, but there's nothing very deep or humanly attractive about their fraternity.

NHAT HANH: Remember the time you told me about a friend in Hanoi who said he could identify the Catholics by the look in their eyes? I think those believers belong to the period of time when people had no doubt concerning the way that had been prescribed. It is not very easy to find people like that in our times.

I have meditated on these problems, and I have seen that the notion of the *way* is very misleading. Most people think a way presupposes a distance and is like a rope linking one to a point in space, in time. Between two points, there is a distance and a link. When we detect a way to arrive at our destination, it is as though we made reservations on a flight.

But it is commonly thought that we remain the same, here and there. That is not the case, I believe. Because if you are not transformed on the way, you remain at the point of departure all the time; you never arrive at the destination. So, the way must be *in you*; the destination also must be in you and not somewhere else in space or time. If that kind of self-transformation is being realized in you, you *will* arrive. But if you remain the same, no plane can bring you to the point of arrival.

In the old time, in times when they were too sure of the way, people believed that there was a prescribed formula, a prescribed way. You only engaged in it, believed it, took the risk of belief, and you were transported along. In saying this, I'm not denying that man has to take the Law into account, that he has to rely on God, on Buddha. That is not the problem I'm talking about here. I'm thinking only of the misleading nature of the word *way*, which implies a destination. And it also implies the rejection of something and the embrace of something else. To me, that difference doesn't exist. The difference is merely a way of looking at this world. In Buddhist terms this very world in Nirvana; it depends on you. The way is in your mind; it is your way.

I want to express my hope in the community of people who have the same concerns and who are working for the same goals. What helps individuals in the community is your doing the same things I do, in your own way. I can learn from you. I feel the need of your presence. Not only because I have a feeling of physical loneliness, but I feel that I need you in many other respects: sharing of experiences, the support of each other in difficult moments (difficult moments not only understood as financial or political difficulties). Difficulties here might be purely in spiritual or religious terms, because in the life of a man who lives his religion, there are crises, and these crises are not only destructive, but very constructive, to destroy in order to build. That process of destruction-creation brings us ahead in our process of self-realization. So, the friend is at your side, even if he does nothing for you during this period of crisis, even if he says nothing to comfort you. The way he looks at you is something you need. There was one time when I underwent a crisis, and with me there was only a cat to look at me; and that helped a lot.

BERRIGAN: I think most of the communities that are staying together have this view that you speak of, a particular view of the way. That was a great word of Jesus about Himself, "I am the way." And also in the Acts of the Apostles, the early Christians always spoke of their faith as "the way." I've often thought of the people who are on the way, all the people I met recently in the Middle East. I meditate on their lives, their attitudes as they spoke to us, and it seems to me it makes no sense to be on one's way and yet act as though one had arrived. At least to a degree, one should be as content about this stage as though it were the last stage. Perhaps even more important, one should contain within himself all the necessary purity and love which signalize the end.

Gandhi often spoke of making the means equivalent to the end, so that one would not do anything today that would disperse or distract or corrupt what one is trying to move toward. That is perhaps one way of putting the greatness of the saints and of those we admire, that their lives contain the end in the very movement toward it.

NHAT HANH: Very deep and true. I think that "I am the way" is much, much better than a statement like "I know the way." See, "I am the way," the way is more than an asphalt surface.

BERRIGAN: Or more than a road map.

NHAT HANH: A road map! But I would make a distinction between the "I" in the phrase spoken by Jesus and the "I" that people may think of. The "I" in His statement is much, much larger and closer; not closer, it is life itself, His life! "I am the way." His life, which *is* life, is the way. If you don't look, if you don't really look at His life, you cannot see the way. But if you only satisfy yourself with the name, with saying a name, even if that name is Jesus, it is not the life of Jesus. The way should be understood as Jesus Himself and not just a few notions one has concerning His appearance.

BERRIGAN: I remember the movie of Pasolini, *The Gospel of*

St. Matthew. Jesus is always in motion; He teaches while He's walking with His friends. And He's always walking very quickly, never seated somewhere; He's walking, and speaking over His shoulder while they're trying to keep up with Him. I thought this was not just a striking way of showing the urgency of the truth; it went deeper than that. It was as though life itself is a forward movement of awareness, of consciousness, of love; and He's dramatizing this by moving. His life is a movement, and they can't remain static and hope to grasp what He is about. They cannot remain in comfort; they cannot remain in the past. It's as though He's a kind of spool which is unwinding; they're trying to grab it as it goes, but it's always going. Or He's a great fish that they've caught; and yet He's not caught and they have to keep trying to draw Him to them. The fishing line always keeps unwinding ahead of them, because He's still ahead of them, and because He contains the whole thing. Even though they can only take in part of it, they must keep moving to grasp even that part.

So much "sacred" art has snuffed out the spirit of Jesus. He sits there in heavenly rest, tossing them words which they accept passively. But in Pasolini's movie there's a kind of uneasy motion, an effort to hear, and maybe not to hear all of it. Maybe the wind carries part of it away; but they just have to keep moving in order to hear Him, for the teaching is not static. The same physical effort required to stay with Him on the road is required to stay with Him in spirit.

NHAT HANH: The teaching is not static because it is not mere words; it is the reality of life. There are those who have neither the way nor the life. They try to impose on others what they believe to be the way, but it is only words that have no connection with real life, a real way.

BERRIGAN: I often thought, What a privilege Merton had in his community. It's something I never had—a group of brothers of all ages and of all degrees of understanding, to live with them over long, long periods of time. Even at the edge of it, as he often was, and dissatisfied with many aspects of it, it was still a great source of satisfaction for him, as well as a rare grace. I was going over some of his letters recently, before I came to Paris, and I had a new sense of the suffering the community caused him, especially in the repressive efforts of superiors to censor some of his writing. And yet, I think I learned not so much what the community did for him, but that his suffering, acceptance, and understanding helped him grow in stature. I remember, too, difficult periods in my own order, when I would open up freely to him. His word was always, "We must stay where we are. We must stay with our community, even though it's absurd, makes no sense, and causes great suffering." He felt that the times were so chaotic, and people so quickly destroyed, that it was important to stand firm. He helped me in that way many times.

I think in the sixties he went through some of the worst times I ever witnessed among my friends. Yet he kept a deep understanding of the vitality a human being draws from his brothers and sisters. I often think that in my order part of my responsibility is parallel to his own: to keep a strong appreciation of the community, especially when so many are tempted to give up.

There is something mysterious in the timing of people or in projects. When we were in prison, there was a strong community. And everyone said, "We must get together when we get out because the war is still on and there's still work to do." So when we were released, we tried, but it was a disaster. Suddenly, we found that we were very different. People were moving in other directions; people were forming other relationships. People who got along in jail were now very difficult toward one another. After less than a year, this community of ex-prisoners just broke up. But now we find through letters that some are quietly coming together in Washington. Maybe it took all that time, two years or more, for the real thing to happen. Maybe the real thing just continues to happen.